Sharing Your Faith and Testimony

Trusting God Fully and Completely

Pastor S. Alfred Cherubim

Redeemer Christ Assembly
Brampton

Sharing Your Faith and Testimony

Alfred Cherubim

2023 © by Alfred Cherubim

All rights reserved. Published 2023.

BIBLE SCRIPTURES

SHARING YOUR
FAITH
— AND —
TESTIMONY

ALFRED CHERUBIM

Printed in the United States of America

Spirit Media and our logos are trademarks of Spirit Media

ॐ SPIRIT MEDIA

www.spiritmedia.us
1249 Kildaire Farm Rd STE 112
Cary, NC 27511
1 (888) 800-3744

Books › Christian Books & Bibles › Christian Living

Paperback ISBN: 978-1-961614-78-9
Hardback ISBN: 978-1-961614-79-6
Audiobook ISBN: 978-1-961614-80-2
eBook ISBN: 978-1-961614-77-2
Library of Congress Control Number: 2023918781

*This book is dedicated to glorify God,
for His grace and mercies provided for me to
serve Him these 40 long years.*

Table of Contents

Introduction

Meet Pastor Alfred Cherubim, a Sri Lankan now living in Canada. His life is a testimony to the incredible power of faith as he experienced miraculous encounters with Jesus Christ. These encounters changed his life and inspired a mission to share the message of Jesus with the world.

In the pages ahead, you'll journey through continents and cultures. Through the story of Pastor Cherubim and his family, you'll witness the incredible impact of saving faith and the enduring message of Christ's love. This book isn't just about one man's extraordinary experiences; it's an invitation to explore the timeless truths of the Gospel.

Once we personally meet the Savior, we're never again the same. We cannot keep it quiet. And in today's world, sharing our testimony about Jesus Christ is more important than ever. Testimonies show how faith can transform lives. It's not just storytelling; it's a powerful act. It invites others to witness the life-changing power of Christ, find joy in salvation, and start their own spiritual journeys.

SHARING YOUR FAITH AND TESTIMONY

PART 2

Testify & Glorify

Our Testimony

I was born in Jaffna, Sri Lanka, to Philip Devasagayam Savarimuttu and Mary Ann. I attended St. Patrick's College in Jaffna and later worked as an Agricultural Instructor in the Department of Agriculture. After leaving government service, I joined the National Council of the YMCAs of Sri Lanka as the Director of the Youth Training Centre in Paranthan. In 1981, I became the Associate National General Secretary of the National YMCA in Colombo, Sri Lanka.

While I was serving in Paranthan, my wife became seriously ill and fell into a coma. She spent nearly three months in Jaffna Hospital under the care of a team of three doctors from the Medical Faculty. Despite their best efforts, they were unable to improve her condition, and her health continued to deteriorate. After conducting examinations, the doctors advised me to take her home because no further treatment could help, and they believed she had only two weeks left to live.

Doctors & Medicines Failed

During that period, we brought her home, expecting her to pass away soon. It was during these difficult days that Pastor Santhanapillai from the Church of Prayer in Paranthan came and shared the message of God's love and the miraculous power of Jesus with me.

Although I was a Christian, my understanding of God was distant, not personal. Another three months passed, but there was no improvement in her health while we kept her at home.

During this time, Evangelist Bro. S. Rajandram from Jesus Lives Ministry in Colombo was conducting a healing crusade in our town. Pastor Santhanapillai suggested bringing him to pray for my wife's healing. Initially, I was reluctant because I wanted only our church members involved due to our traditions and faith rituals. However, I agreed thanks to Pastor Santhanapillai's love and insistence.

Again, I was unwilling to provide them transportation in my car. Instead, I arranged for my official vehicle and driver, as I lacked faith and didn't hold much regard for them or believe in their prayers. My loyalty was more towards the church and its hierarchy than towards God. On that day, these servants of God eventually came to my house on their own. They prayed for my wife with tears and a heavy heart for a few minutes, offered me comfort, and then left.

Jesus Never Fails

What a wonder! Immediately after they left, within just minutes, my wife, who had been unconscious in a coma for nearly six months, miraculously woke up, completely normal, and resumed her usual household tasks on the same day. God answered the fervent prayer of His servant and instantly healed my wife.

Again, I was thrilled by the healing but had no curiosity about the Healer. I didn't even think to call and thank the Evangelist or the Pastor who had prayed for my wife; my heart was hard. However, Jesus showed His love by performing three more powerful miracles in our family, one after the other.

Six months after my wife's healing, I suffered a heart attack. I underwent treatment, which included dietary restrictions and light work, along with regular check-ups with a cardiologist. About nine months after my wife's recovery, the same evangelist organized another healing crusade in our town. This time, I made the choice to attend one of their meetings to see what was happening there.

The meeting was held in a school hall with more than three hundred attendees. As the evening grew darker, I entered the hall cautiously and positioned myself at the back rows, trying to avoid being noticed because I didn't want my fellow church members to know I was at such an event. I was more concerned about people seeing me rather than realizing that God was watching over me.

Prophesy and Healing

During the meeting, the evangelist preached about healing from the Word of God. I was more interested in observing what would happen than in his message. After the sermon, he started prophesying, accurately describing the health issues of several people. Eventually, he turned to me and gave a detailed prophecy about my heart attack and even described the clothes I was wearing, making it clear that the message was for me.

He then invited those to whom he had prophesied to come forward for prayers. All seven or eight people stepped forward, but I held back, feeling shy and not wanting to be in front of such a crowd. Deep down, though, I knew that God had called me through His servant. I now had faith that the same God who had miraculously lifted my wife from her death bed could also heal me.

In my heart, I prayed, "Lord Jesus, I believe you called me. I know you can heal me now. Please forgive me for not coming forward and my unfamiliarity with these types of prayer meetings..." Then the Brother on stage began to pray for all the sick individuals present. At that moment, I felt an electric shock pass through my entire body, a heaviness lift from my chest, and an overwhelming sense of joy and happiness that I had never experienced before in my life. I knew I was instantly healed. What a glorious experience! The power of God touched me like lightning!

People who were healed were asked to go on stage and share their testimonies to praise God. Many of them walked up and began talking about their healing experiences.

Once again, I chose not to step forward and give my testimony to glorify God. Instead, I walked out and went home. I was happy with my healing and didn't feel the need to acknowledge the Healer, Jesus.

Ten lepers came to Jesus, and they were cured of their leprosy. However, only one of them returned to Jesus to give glory to God, while the other nine left after being healed, without returning to give thanks. Similarly, I was like one of those nine lepers; I received my healing and went away without acknowledging or praising God.

I returned to my regular worldly life, keeping our healing experience a secret, even from the evangelist who prayed for us. What a stony, hard-hearted man I was! My heart had grown hard because I was determined to stick to my traditions and rituals, avoiding outside influences.

During this time, I received a promotion at the YMCA and became the Deputy National General Secretary, working at the Colombo National Office. I was more interested in my position and worldly recognition than in knowing God or growing in my spiritual life.

Another Miracle

Our good Lord did not forsake me despite my unfaithfulness. He had a plan to draw my family closer to Him and performed another miracle. This time, it was my youngest daughter, who was five years old at the time, suffering from severe eczema and sores covering her body from her hips to her toes. There wasn't a single spot on her body without sores. She endured immense pain, had sleepless nights, cried most of the time, and remained restless throughout the day.

Again, we tried the best medications and consulted multiple doctors, even exploring local native treatments. All these failed and nearly three months passed without any trace of improvement. My daughter missed her schooling and studies during this time. That's when I thought of the evangelist who had prayed for my wife and me and decided to seek his prayers for my daughter's healing.

Since the servant of God lived in Colombo City, where we also resided, I called him and asked him to come and pray for my child. This humble servant of God promptly agreed and arrived at our home within hours. He saw my daughter's condition, comforted us with the Word of God, anointed her with oil, and encouraged us to continue praying for her.

Having witnessed the miraculous power of prayer in both my wife and me, we had faith that Jesus, who had healed us, could also cure our daughter through fervent prayers. So, we stopped her medication and began praying, using oil in the name of Jesus. From the first day, we noticed improvement, and within ten days, she was completely healed.

Praise God! Medicines and doctors failed, but Jesus never did. We were so happy, and as our daughter returned to school, everything seemed fine. However, there was no change in my heart. I remained the same, unfaithful, and only concerned about our healing and well-being. I failed to express my gratitude to God for His mighty miracles, or to the person who came to our home and prayed earnestly for our healing.

Compassionate God

God, in His great mercy, had compassion on my family and me. He extended His loving hand to perform His fourth miracle for someone like me, who lacked faith.

This time, my eldest daughter, who was fifteen years old at the time, fell ill with chronic rheumatic paralysis. She had swelling in all her joints from her neck to her feet, rendering her unable to walk. She suffered severe pain and remained bedridden for two and a half months. We sought the best treatment in Colombo City through my YMCA contacts, but despite taking 25 to 30 painkiller tablets daily, her health didn't improve.

Apart from our daughter's physical suffering, as parents, we endured significant mental stress and strain watching our growing child confined to a bed for days with no improvement despite all the medication. At this point, I had no choice but to reach out to the same servant of God who had prayed for me, my wife, and our youngest daughter. I sought his prayers for the healing of our eldest daughter, as all other treatments had failed, and she couldn't bear the rheumatic pains any longer.

On the evening of December 24th (Christmas Eve), I called the same evangelist Brother to come and pray for our daughter. He arrived, prayed with deep devotion, and left. What a marvelous move of God! Shortly after he left, our daughter, who had been bedridden for almost three months, miraculously jumped out of bed and started walking and running as if she had never been sick.

Opened My Heart to Jesus

Oh, we couldn't believe our eyes at first, but it was real! It was at that moment my heart was deeply moved, and with tears, I asked God for forgiveness for my unfaithfulness. I also wanted to learn more about this Healer. On the same night, my wife, children, and I went to the worship place of this servant of God, which was his house at the time. We attended the midnight Christmas service and, for the first time in our lives, shared our testimony of all the miracles that God had performed for us through the prayers of this servant of God.

On December 24th, 1980, at midnight, my wife and I accepted Jesus as our personal Savior.

What a joyful experience it was to come to know our Lord in a personal way! I realized how hard-hearted I had been. However, our good Lord performed four mighty and wonderful miracles in me and my family, which softened my stony heart and allowed me to discover the tender heart of Jesus.

All of this happened within a year, and after these experiences, we committed our lives to Jesus, got baptized, and began attending a church in Colombo. There, we focused ourselves on studying God's Word, spent time in fasting and prayer, joined Vigil night prayer meetings, participated in foot-washing ceremonies, helped with evangelical meetings and crusades, and took part in various ministry activities. During this time, I received a powerful anointing from the Holy Spirit, which gave me wisdom to understand the Bible and revealed important truths. This strengthened my faith to totally surrender my life to serve Him.

First Sermon on Job

Three glorious years passed as a born-again Christian, growing in faith and favor with God. During this time, Brother Rajandram, the founder of "Jesus Lives Ministry," where my entire family and I attended as regular members, asked me to preach on a specific Sunday. He was leaving for an evangelical mission in India and trusted me as an elder of his church. At first, I hesitated and felt unworthy to stand and preach at his pulpit, where God had used him mightily to perform miracles and preach the Word with authority and power. However, as a humble servant, he reminded me that God can use anyone for His glory if we fully and completely submit our lives into His mighty hands. After praying and entrusting me with the responsibility to preach that particular Sunday, he left for India.

Taking on the responsibility to preach, I dedicated several days to fasting and prayer, seeking God's guidance and strength for the task ahead. The Holy Spirit clearly and powerfully directed me to speak from the Book of Job. That entire week, I spent hours on my knees studying Job's life, taking notes, and preparing for my first-ever sermon. It was a significant moment for me, especially since I was preaching in a Spirit-filled church where the miraculous power of God was a common experience for those attending every service.

It was Sunday, July 24th, 1983, the appointed day for my first sermon. On that day, I attended church with my wife and three children. After the worship and sharing time, I stood up to preach for the first time. I spoke about the life of Job and encouraged everyone present to be like him, always thanking God no matter the circumstances, whether in times of gain or loss.

As Job said in 1:21, "Naked I came from my mother's womb, and naked I will depart. The Lord gave and the Lord has taken away; may the name of the Lord be praised."(NIV). I repeated these words and emphasized to the congregation that even if we lose everything in our lives, we must still maintain our trust in God and depend on Him, just as Job did when he said, "Even if he slays me, I will hope in him" (NET). I also added that the same God who blessed Job with twice as much as he had before would also bless us when we completely and fully trust in Him.

Becoming Job

I preached about Job on Sunday, and the very next day, Sri Lanka experienced its worst ethnic riots. The conflict between the Sri Lankan Government and the Tamil movement, seeking the rights of the minority Tamils, escalated that day, resulting in the largest riots the country had ever witnessed. Hundreds and thousands of Tamils were killed and tortured. Vehicles, houses, shops, factories, and all possessions belonging to Tamil people living in Sinhalese areas were burnt down. I, too, became a victim of this riot when our house and all our belongings were burnt to ashes on that fateful day.

On that Monday, the government imposed a curfew throughout the entire country. I had to leave the office, and my children rushed back from school. We were all confined to our home, behind closed doors, not knowing what was happening outside. Our only weapons for protection were PRAYER and the WORD OF GOD. We had our Bibles with us and were reading and meditating. It was around 5:00 pm. My sister's family and my niece's family, who lived in the adjoining annex of our house, joined us to stay together during this calamity. We knelt down and began to pray. I prayed, submitting everyone into God's hands for our safety and protection. Shortly after we finished praying, we heard the sound of breaking glass and people shouting from our neighbor's house. We rushed to one of our washrooms in the bedroom to hide for safety. Within minutes, a mob broke down our doors and entered our house.

There were a total of thirteen of us, including children, hiding in that washroom and praying. The mob that entered our house, numbering about 10–12 people as we could tell from their voices, ransacked our home for nearly two hours. They broke doors, windows, TVs, the fridge, chairs, tables, and more. Eventually, they reached the room where we were hiding. First, they searched that room and attempted to enter the washroom. However, since it was latched from the inside, they couldn't open it. They resorted to smashing that simple door with an iron bar several times, but it remained intact. Incredible! What a wonder! This was the moment we witnessed and experienced the mighty power of God literally protecting us from danger.

God lifted us from Fire

After causing all possible damage to our house and belongings, the mob assumed that there were no people inside and left. After two hours of fearful threats and violence, the house fell into silence. We thought the worst was over. However, we soon saw bombs being thrown from the road, and our sitting hall caught fire. We rushed out of the house through a rear door into the courtyard, not knowing what to do. Behind us, the entire house was now fully engulfed in flames. Our only escape seemed to be over an eleven-foot parapet wall that separated our property from our neighbor's. But it was too high to jump, and the wall was narrow, only about a foot and a half wide and made of plastered brick. The fire was getting closer to us, just a few feet away.

In this crucial moment, when everyone around was shaken and frightened, God granted me an unknown strength and courage. I felt no fear at that particular moment. With the Bible in my hand (which I had taken to the washroom for protection), I struck the parapet wall, declaring, "In the Name of Jesus, I break this wall." Miraculously, the entire wall, just above our hip level, fell onto the other side, allowing us to cross over to our neighbor's property and escape from the burning fire. It was yet another powerful display of God's protection that we saw and experienced right before our eyes.

"For by you I can run against a troop. And by my God I can leap over a wall."

– Psalm 18:29 (ESV)

Throughout that night, we stayed at our loving neighbor's house, who helped us in various ways. However, in the early hours after midnight, the government army and the mob started searching houses one by one, seeking Tamil individuals sheltered by friendly Sinhalese families. If found, they were killed. Fortunately, our neighbor had informed the police of our situation and advised us to return to our burnt house, where we could hide among the debris on our land, avoiding the army and the violent mob.

Miraculous Ladder

In the early hours of the following morning, we wanted to return to our land across the broken wall. This required some climbing because our neighbor's land was lower than ours. We began organizing a way to climb the wall, especially for the women and children. To our surprise, we discovered a brand new bamboo ladder placed near the wall. Our neighbor friend didn't own such a ladder, and it was completely new. Additionally, it was the exact height needed to reach the broken wall. Without any difficulty, we used the ladder to reach our land until the police arrived to escort us to the police station for our safety that early morning.

What a mighty God we serve! He is our provider, and He miraculously provided us with a ladder seemingly out of nowhere. This was yet another powerful demonstration of our good Lord's protection by supplying our immediate need – a ladder.

On that day, every police station was overwhelmed with affected Tamils, and the government established refugee camps to accommodate them. Like many others, we were taken to one of these refugee camps, which quickly filled up with nearly ten thousand people from the surrounding areas shortly after our arrival.

The Lord Gave, the Lord has Taken

At the camp, the first thing I did was to take my wife and three children aside and kneel down in prayer. I thanked God for all the protection He had provided us and quoted Job 1:21, **"Naked I came from my mother's womb, and naked I will depart. The Lord gave and the Lord has taken away; may the name of the Lord be praised"** (NIV). I also made a promise to God that because He had performed mighty wonders and miracles for me, my wife, and children, I would share our testimonies with tears for His glory wherever I had the opportunity.

We had to stay in the refugee camp for approximately two weeks, where we sat and slept on the floor. We had lost everything we owned in our lives, except for the clothes on our backs and my English Bible that I had taken with me when I rushed to the washroom for protection.

My wife had left her Tamil Bible in the washroom where we hid while escaping our burning house. She was able to recover her Bible after two and a half months because the washroom was untouched by the fire. We were left with only our Bibles, which we saw as a sign to go and share the Word of God. I began my witnessing within the camp itself.

Starting my Evangelical Ministry

On Sunday, July 24th, 1983, I preached about Job. The very next day, Monday, July 25th, I experienced a situation similar to Job's. By Tuesday, July 26th, we were in a refugee camp, and it was there that I began my evangelistic ministry following my first Spirit-guided sermon on "JOB."

In 1984, we settled in Jaffna for a while since Colombo wasn't safe, and our children were scared after witnessing our house and belongings being burnt down. However, staying in Jaffna became increasingly challenging due to the ongoing turmoil in the country. Even the Tamil homeland was not secure due to the army's atrocities. Reluctantly, we had no choice but to leave Sri Lanka and seek refuge in India.

The Indian YMCA welcomed us, and I was appointed as a full-fledged Secretary in Hyderabad/Secunderabad YMCA in Andhra Pradesh. While serving the YMCA, I continued my evangelical ministry for the three years we lived there. I visited many villages, testifying about the miracles that God had performed in our lives, and preaching the Word of God. As a result of this effort, twelve people accepted Jesus as their personal Savior and were baptized. Two of these individuals, who had experienced the miraculous power of God during that time, are now full-time pastors who have established churches in the area, and God is using them mightily. I thank God and praise Him for His mercies.

While in India, God promoted me to become one of the National YMCA Executive Secretaries. Unusually, I was placed in the New Delhi National Office as the head of two departments. This position allowed me to travel officially to various parts of India, where I was able to share my testimony and preach during weekends and off-hours. Normally, as a non-citizen, I wouldn't have held such an executive role in the Indian YMCA movement. However, in His own way, God removed all obstacles, and I was included in the National Cadre of Secretaries, approved by the National Board of the Indian YMCA, making history for His glory. I cannot explain how it all happened, but I only know that "But with God everything is possible"(Matthew 19:26, NLT).

Starting the Children's Home and Church

In 1990, we returned to Sri Lanka and settled in Trincomalee. There, I established a children's home called **"COME HOME,"** which stands for "**C**hildren **O**ut of **M**otherly **E**mbrace – **H**ope **O**ffered with **M**aternal **E**nfold."

This home was created for children who had lost their parents during the riots. We cared for fifty-three boys aged four to twelve, raising them alongside our own three children. We provided them with education and nurtured them in the fear of God. During this time, I also founded the "Jesus Lives Prayer Fellowship" church, and through this ministry, we reached out to many souls. As a result of our ministry and the children's home, three children from our care have become pastors, serving the Lord in Trincomalee today. What a mighty God we serve! All praise and glory belong to our good Lord, who made all of this possible.

Ministry abroad

In 1996, God opened doors for me to engage in foreign mission work when the German YMCA invited me to share our testimony and preach among the youth of the YMCA there. This invitation came about because some youths who had visited our Children's Home in Sri Lanka were encouraged by their experience during their stay with us in Trincomalee. This opportunity allowed me to visit several other countries during that trip. Thereafter, it became an annual program, and between 1996 and 2001, I visited several countries multiple times, including India, England, Germany, France, Denmark, Norway, Switzerland, Netherlands, Belgium, Canada, America, and Australia. During these visits, I shared our miraculous testimonies, preached the Word of God, and offered encouragement to pastors, believers, and others in Tamil and English churches in these countries.

In 2001, a crucial year brought about many changes in our lives. My wife and I had plans to visit several countries, as we had obtained the necessary visas. However, our journey began in Canada, where we intended to join our children. Unfortunately, during my usual preaching mission in Canada, I suffered a severe heart attack. This health crisis forced us to remain in Canada for medical treatment, as I was in no condition to travel further.

Redeemer Christ Assembly in Brampton

The Canadian Government allowed us to stay in Canada due to our circumstances. I didn't choose a relaxed life but remained active in my ministry. Today, I am the Pastor of "Redeemer Christ Assembly" in Brampton, reaching out to people in this city and beyond. By God's grace, we have a TV Ministry, Newspaper Ministry, Booklet publication, and I'm pleased to have released this book, "Sharing Your Faith & Testimony," for the glory of our good Lord and Savior Jesus Christ.

Testify and Glorify

Dear Brothers! And Sisters!!

I hope and pray that this book, "Sharing Your Faith & Testimony," will encourage and strengthen you to become a tool in God's hands, bringing glory to His Holy name through your life. Every believer is called to do so. Together, let us faithfully witness and bring many souls into His fold.

> "Bring all who claim me as their God, for I have made them for my glory. It was I who created them."
>
> – Isaiah 43:7 (NLT)

In the words of Isaiah, we find a profound message about our purpose and identity as individuals created by God. Isaiah 43:7 reminds us that each of us is called by His name, crafted with care, and designed for His glory. It's a beautiful reminder that our existence has a divine purpose, and in living out that purpose, we bring glory to God.

> "But you are my witnesses, O Israel!" says the Lord. "You are my servant. You have been chosen to know me, believe in me, and understand that I alone am God.There is no other God—there never has been,

and there never will be. I, yes I, am the Lord, and there is no other Savior. First I predicted your rescue, then I saved you and proclaimed it to the world. No foreign god has ever done this. You are witnesses that I am the only God," says the Lord.

— Isaiah 43:10-12 (NLT)

We are God's witnesses, chosen to know, believe, and understand Him (Isaiah 43:10-12). There is no other God besides Him, and He is the one and only Savior. We are called to declare His uniqueness and the fact that He is God, the One who has declared, saved, and proclaimed His presence.

"I have made Israel for myself, and they will someday honor me before the whole world."

— Isaiah 43:21 (NLT)

Isaiah 43:21 further emphasizes our place in God's divine plan. He has shaped us to proclaim His praise. This verse highlights that our existence serves as a testament to His greatness, and our mission is to honor and glorify Him through our lives.

Therefore, let us pray for the guidance and power of the Holy Spirit to testify of and to glorify our God. May our good Lord guard you, guide you, and lead you to serve Him. Glorify HIM, and HIM only!

S. Alfred Cherubim
Pastor
Redeemer Christ Assembly
Brampton, Ontario L6R 1L2
CANADA

Sharing our Faith

God has called every believer to share their faith in Him with others who may not know Him, allowing them to come to the knowledge of Him and accept Jesus Christ as their personal Savior through faith, receiving the free gift of salvation that believers already enjoy.

The privilege of sharing Jesus with others is reserved for human beings alone. Among all of God's creation, including animals, birds, fish, and even the angels in Heaven, it's our responsibility to share the Gospel; the choice is ours to make, whether to share or to refuse.

Tell your story. Let others know what your life was like before you found Christ, and the peace and joy you now experience, knowing your sins are forgiven. You're now living according to God's purpose for you and have the hope of everlasting life. Sharing your personal experience and relationship with Jesus Christ, with sincerity and conviction, can be a powerful way to witness to some people.

Sharing our Faith Effectively

"and I pray that the sharing of your faith may become effective for the full knowledge of every good thing that is in us for the sake of Christ."

– Philemon 1:6 (ESV)

Philemon 1:6 reminds us of the power of sharing our faith. When we acknowledge the goodness that resides within us through Christ Jesus, our ability to share our faith becomes more effective. It's a beautiful reminder that our faith has the potential to positively impact others when we recognize the goodness that Christ has instilled in us.

These words bring to mind several other verses of Scripture. "Acknowledging every good thing..." indicates that we are to share our faith in the spirit of thanksgiving, giving thanks to the Lord for all that He has done for us, all that He is doing for us, and all that He will do for us. When we find it difficult to share our faith, we must learn to stand upon God's Word.

> "Thanks be to God, who gives us the victory through our Lord Jesus Christ."

> - 1 Corinthians 15:57 (ESV)

The verse from 1 Corinthians 15:57 is a wonderful expression of gratitude. It reminds us to give thanks to God, recognizing that it is through our Lord Jesus Christ that we receive victory. This victory encompasses both the spiritual triumph over sin and the assurance of eternal life. It's a powerful reminder of the blessings and grace that come through our faith in Christ.

> "for God gave us a spirit not of fear but of power and love and self-control."

> – 2 Timothy 1:7 (ESV)

In times of uncertainty or when faced with fear, the words of 2 Timothy 1:7 offer comfort and strength. They serve as a reminder that as believers, we are not meant to be dominated by fear. Instead, we are given a spirit characterized by power, love, and a sound mind. This verse encourages us to approach life's challenges with confidence and faith, knowing that God equips us with the tools we need to overcome fear and walk in His light.

When we effectively share our faith, it's crucial to remember this:

"This is the Lord's doing; it is marvelous in our eyes."

– Psalm 118:23 (ESV)

This must be our testimony:

"Not to us, O Lord, not to us, but to your name give glory, for the sake of your steadfast love and your faithfulness!"

– Psalm 115:1 (ESV)

When we effectively share our faith, it's crucial to remember the wisdom of Psalm 118:23. The work we do in spreading the message of the Lord is truly marvelous and is a reflection of His divine plan. Our testimony should echo the sentiments of Psalm 115:1, acknowledging that the glory belongs to the Lord and His Name. It is by His mercy and truth that we carry out this mission of sharing His love and message with others. Let these verses guide and inspire our efforts in the service of God.

If we are to be effective witnesses for Christ, we must learn to "abide in Christ," never forgetting that: "without Him we can do nothing." "Abiding in Christ" (John 15:7) is the way we bear much fruit.

May the Word of God dwell richly in my heart from hour to hour, so that all may see I triumph only through His power.

There will be times when we need to share our faith with people going through difficult times. To truly help them, we should pray for our own faith to be strong so we can share the Lord's strength with them.

"May the peace of God my Father rule my heart in everything, that I may be calm to comfort the sick and sorrowful."

Sharing our faith effectively means sharing the love of Jesus. We should pray that His love shines through us as we witness for Him.

"May the love of Jesus fill me, as the waters fill the sea; Him exalting, self abasing, this is victory."

Created to Glorify God

"I will say to the north, 'Give them up!' and to the south, 'Do not hold them back.' Bring my sons from afar and my daughters from the ends of the earth— everyone who is called by my name, whom I created for my glory, whom I formed and made."

– Isaiah 43: 6-7 (NIV)

"I, even I, am the Lord, and apart from me there is no savior. I have revealed and saved and proclaimed—I, and not some foreign god among you. You are my witnesses," declares the Lord, "that I am God."

– Isaiah 43:11-12 (NIV)

"the people I formed for myself that they may proclaim my praise."

– Isaiah 43:21 (NIV)

Isaiah 43 (verses 6-7, 11-12, 21) paints a beautiful picture of God's calling and purpose for His people. In these verses, we see God's divine intention to gather His sons and daughters from all corners of the earth, regardless of their origins. He calls us by name, not because of anything we've done, but because He has created us for His glory. It's a powerful reminder that our existence is intricately tied to God's purpose, and we are uniquely formed to reflect His glory.

God emphasizes that He is the one and only Savior. He has demonstrated His saving power time and again, and there is no other god or savior besides Him. We are His witnesses, tasked with the incredible responsibility of declaring to the world that He alone is God.

In the grand tapestry of God's plan, we are a people uniquely formed by Him for the purpose of declaring His praise. Our lives are meant to be a testimony to His greatness and His work in us. These verses inspire us to embrace our role in God's plan with humility and gratitude, recognizing that our ultimate purpose is to bring glory to His name.

Dear Brother & Sister in Christ!

God created us in His image to glorify His name and bear witness that He is the only God. Our purpose is to declare His praise.

> "I am writing to all of you in Rome who are loved by God and are called to be his own holy people. Let me say first that I thank my God through Jesus Christ for all of you, because your faith in him is being talked about all over the world."
>
> –Romans 1:7-8 (NLT)

In Romans 1:7-8, Paul warmly addresses the Christians in Rome, calling them beloved of God and saints. He expresses gratitude for their well-known faith, emphasizing its impact on the world. These verses highlight the importance of grace and peace from God the Father and the Lord Jesus Christ, uniting believers in fellowship.

Witness to all the Nations

"And the Good News about the Kingdom will be preached throughout the whole world, so that all nations will hear it; and then the end will come."

– Matthew 24:14 (NLT)

In fulfillment of Jesus' teaching in Matthew 24:14, our mission is clear: to spread the gospel across the globe. This act of witnessing serves as a powerful testament to the transformative power of God's Word in our lives and its potential to bring faith and salvation to people from every corner of the world. It marks an important milestone in God's divine plan before the end times.

"God sent a man, John the Baptist, to tell about the light so that everyone might believe because of his testimony. John himself was not the light; he was simply a witness to tell about the light.The one who is the true light, who gives light to everyone, was coming into the world."

– John 1:6-9 (NLT)

John the Baptist, was a man sent by God to bear witness to the Light, which is Jesus Christ. (John 1:6-9) John's role was not to be the Light but to testify about the true Light, whose purpose was to bring illumination and faith to every person in the world.

"not to the general public, but to us whom God had chosen in advance to be his witnesses. We were those who ate and drank with him after he rose from the dead. And he ordered us to preach everywhere and to testify that Jesus is the one appointed by God to be the judge of all—the living and the dead. He is the one all the prophets testified about, saying that everyone who believes in him will have their sins forgiven through his name."

– Acts 10:41-43 (NLT)

The Scriptures in Acts 10:41-43 remind us that as witnesses chosen by God, early Christians had the wonderful privilege of dining with Jesus after His resurrection. He entrusted them with the vital mission of preaching to the people and bearing witness that He is the one ordained by God to judge the living and the dead. This message, supported by the testimony of the prophets, proclaims that through faith in His name, anyone can find forgiveness for their sins.

"But you will receive power when the Holy Spirit comes upon you. And you will be my witnesses, telling people about me everywhere—in Jerusalem, throughout Judea, in Samaria, and to the ends of the earth."

– Acts 1:8 (NLT)

We have been given the same mission, and in Acts 1:8, we are reminded of the promise of the Holy Spirit, who empowers us to be witnesses of Jesus not only in our immediate surroundings but also to the farthest reaches of the earth. This divine empowerment enables us to share the message of salvation and be a beacon of His light in our communities and beyond.

Do Not Hold Back

"I am under obligation both to Greeks and to barbarians, both to the wise and to the foolish. So I am eager to preach the gospel to you also who are in Rome. For I am not ashamed of the gospel, for it is the power of God for salvation to everyone who believes, to the Jew first and also to the Greek. For in it the righteousness of God is revealed from faith for faith, as it is written, "The righteous shall live by faith."

– Romans 1:14-17 (ESV)

In Romans 1:14-17, the apostle Paul expressed his deep sense of responsibility to share the gospel with everyone, both the educated and the less educated, the Greeks and the Barbarians. He was eager to preach the gospel in Rome because he understood the incredible power it held. Paul was not ashamed of the gospel of Christ; in fact, he believed it to be the very power of God for the salvation of all who believe. This message revealed the righteousness of God, and it emphasized that the just shall live by faith. Paul's words remind us of the profound impact the gospel can have on people's lives, regardless of their background or status.

Dear brethren, we have a responsibility to share our faith with others, just as the Apostle Paul wrote to the Romans. If we hold back the truth when God, in His manifold mercies, has revealed Himself to us, we may face His wrath. We have no excuse to withhold the truth.

"For the wrath of God is revealed from heaven against all ungodliness and unrighteousness of men, who hold the truth in unrighteousness; Because that which may be known of God is manifest in them; for God hath shewed it unto them. For the invisible things of him from the creation of the world are clearly seen, being understood by the things that are made, even his eternal power and Godhead; so that they are without excuse: Because that, when they knew God, they glorified him not as God, neither were thankful; but became vain in their imaginations, and their foolish heart was darkened."

– Romans 1:18-21 (ESV)

The apostle Paul highlights a profound truth about the human condition in Romans 1:18-21. He speaks of how God's wrath is revealed against ungodliness and unrighteousness among people who suppress the truth in their wrongdoing. Paul points out that God's existence and attributes are evident through His creation, leaving humanity without excuse for not acknowledging Him. Despite having this knowledge, some chose not to glorify God or express gratitude. Instead, they allowed their hearts and minds to be clouded by vain imaginations and darkness. These verses serve as a reminder of the importance of recognizing God's presence and giving Him the honor and gratitude He deserves.

"For if I preach the gospel, that gives me no ground for boasting. For necessity is laid upon me. Woe to me if I do not preach the gospel!"

– 1 Corinthians 9:16 (ESV)

In 1 Corinthians 9:16, the apostle Paul expresses a deep sense of responsibility and calling to preach the gospel. He humbly acknowledges that there's no room for boasting about it; instead, he sees it as a necessity laid upon him. Paul's commitment to sharing the message of the gospel is so strong that he even says, "Woe is unto me if I preach not the gospel!" This verse reflects Paul's unwavering dedication to his mission of spreading the good news of Christ, emphasizing the importance of this calling in his life.

> "For what does the scripture say? "Abraham believed God, and it was credited[a] to him as righteousness."Now to the one who works, his pay is not credited due to grace but due to obligation.But to the one who does not work, but believes in the one who declares the ungodly righteous,his faith is credited as righteousness."
>
> – Romans 4:3-5 (NET)

The Scripture reminds us of the powerful concept of faith in Romans 4:3-5. It looks back to the example of Abraham, who believed in God, and as a result, his faith was counted as righteousness. This passage emphasizes that righteousness is not achieved through our works or efforts; instead, it is attained through faith in the One who justifies the ungodly. It's a reminder that our faith in God's grace and mercy is what truly matters in our journey of righteousness.

> "Therefore, since we have been declared righteous by faith, we have peace with God through our Lord Jesus Christ, through whom we have also obtained access into this grace in which we stand, and we rejoice in the hope of God's glory."
>
> – Romans 5:1-2 (NET)

Romans 5:1-2 tells us that through our faith in Jesus Christ, we are justified and find peace with God. It's through Him that we have access to the grace in which we firmly stand, and this access fills us with hope, a hope that rejoices in the glory of God. These verses remind us of the profound connection between faith, justification, and the hope that sustains us.

What is Faith?

Faith is confidence that someone or something is reliable. Our lives are based on faith. Without it, banks and post offices could not function. Paper money and credit cards (the term "credit" originates from the Latin verb "to believe") would not be accepted.

> "Now faith is confidence in what we hope for and assurance about what we do not see. This is what the ancients were commended for. By faith we understand that the universe was formed at God's command, so that what is seen was not made out of what was visible."
>
> – Hebrews 11:1-3 (NIV)

Hebrews 11 beautifully expresses that faith is the foundation of our hopes and the proof of things beyond our sight. Through faith, the elders in history were commended for their righteousness. This faith also grants us insight into the divine truth that the entire universe was intricately crafted by the Word of God, forming the visible world from the invisible. These verses remind us that faith is the key that unlocks our understanding of God's wondrous creation and His faithful promises (verses 1-3).

> "By faith Abel brought God a better offering than Cain did. By faith he was commended as righteous, when God spoke well of his offerings. And by faith Abel still speaks, even though he is dead."
>
> – Hebrews 11:4 (NIV)

Through faith, Abel offered a sacrifice to God that was pleasing and righteous, in contrast to Cain's offering. Abel's faith was so strong that it earned him a witness of righteousness, with God Himself testifying to the quality of his gifts. Even after Abel's passing, his faith continues to speak to us, reminding us of the enduring impact of a life lived in faith and devotion to God (verse 4).

> "By faith Enoch was taken from this life, so that he did not experience death: "He could not be found, because God had taken him away." For before he was taken, he was commended as one who pleased God. And without faith it is impossible to please God, because anyone who comes to him must believe that he exists and that he rewards those who earnestly seek him."
>
> – Hebrews 11:5-6 (NIV)

The story of Enoch is recalled in verses 5-6. Enoch's faith was so unwavering that he experienced a unique fate – he was translated and did not face death as most do. God was so pleased with Enoch's faith that he found favor in His eyes. The key lesson here is that faith is essential in our relationship with God. Without faith, it is impossible to please Him. To approach God, one must believe not only in His existence but also in His role as a rewarder of those who diligently seek Him. Enoch's story serves as an inspiring reminder of the incredible things that faith can accomplish in our walk with God.

> "By faith Noah, when warned about things not yet seen, in holy fear built an ark to save his family. By his faith he condemned the world and became heir of the righteousness that is in keeping with faith."
>
> – Hebrews 11:7 (NIV)

Through his faith, Noah, forewarned by God about events yet unseen, was motivated by the fear of God to build an ark, ensuring the safety of his family. Through this act, he set himself apart from the rest of the world, and thus inherited the righteousness that comes from faith (verse 7).

> "By faith Abraham, when called to go to a place he would later receive as his inheritance, obeyed and went, even though he did not know where he was going. 9 By faith he made his home in the promised land like a stranger in a foreign country; he lived in tents, as did Isaac and Jacob, who were heirs with him of the same promise."
>
> – Hebrews 11:8-9 (NIV)

Guided by faith, Abraham followed the call to venture into an unknown land, destined to be his inheritance, and he obeyed without knowing his destination. In this promised land, he lived as a foreigner, residing in tents alongside Isaac and Jacob, who were co-heirs of this promise (verses 8-9).

> "And by faith even Sarah, who was past childbearing age, was enabled to bear children because she[b] considered him faithful who had made the promise."
>
> – Hebrews 11:11 (NIV)

By her faith, Sara gained the strength to conceive and gave birth to a child, even beyond the usual age for childbearing, because she believed in the faithfulness of the one who had made the promise (verse 11).

> "By faith Abraham, when God tested him, offered Isaac as a sacrifice. He who had embraced the promises was about to sacrifice his one and only son, even though God had said to him, "It is through Isaac that your offspring will be reckoned." Abraham reasoned

> that God could even raise the dead, and so in a manner
> of speaking he did receive Isaac back from death"
>
> — Hebrews 11:17-19 (NIV)

Motivated by faith, Abraham, during his trial, was willing to sacrifice Isaac, his unique son who was the recipient of the promises. He acted on the belief that God, who had declared that Isaac would be the lineage through which his descendants would be named, had the power to resurrect him even from death (verses 17-19).

> "By faith Isaac blessed Jacob and Esau in regard to
> their future"
>
> — Hebrews 11:20 (NIV)

Through his faith, Isaac granted blessings upon his sons, Jacob and Esau, regarding future events (verse 20).

> "By faith Jacob, when he was dying, blessed each of
> Joseph's sons, and worshiped as he leaned on the top
> of his staff."
>
> — Hebrews 11:21 (NIV)

Through his faith, as he approached death, Jacob blessed the two sons of Joseph and worshiped, leaning on his staff (verse 21).

> "By faith Joseph, when his end was near, spoke about
> the exodus of the Israelites from Egypt and gave in-
> structions concerning the burial of his bones."
>
> — Hebrews 11:22 (NIV)

Joseph, in his faith, spoke about the future exodus of the Israelites when he was on his deathbed and gave instructions regarding his remains (verse 22).

> "By faith Moses, when he had grown up, refused to be known as the son of Pharaoh's daughter. He chose to be mistreated along with the people of God rather than to enjoy the fleeting pleasures of sin."
>
> – Hebrews 11:23 (ESV)

Because of their faith, Moses' parents concealed him for three months after his birth, as they recognized his exceptional beauty and were unafraid of the king's decree (verse 23).

> "By faith Moses, when he was come to years, refused to be called the son of Pharaoh's daughter; Choosing rather to suffer affliction with the people of God, than to enjoy the pleasures of sin for a season."
>
> – Hebrews 11:24-25 (NIV)

Once Moses reached adulthood, he deliberately decided not to be identified as the son of Pharaoh's daughter. Instead, he opted to endure hardship alongside the people of God, rejecting the temporary pleasures of sin (verses 24-25).

> "By faith the walls of Jericho fell, after the army had marched around them for seven days."
>
> – Hebrews 11:30 (NIJV)

Through faith, the walls of Jericho collapsed after being encircled for a period of seven days (verse 30).

> "By faith the prostitute Rahab, because she welcomed the spies, was not killed with those who were disobedient."
>
> – Hebrews 11:31 (NIV)

Because of her faith, Rahab the prostitute did not perish along with those who did not believe, as she welcomed the spies in a peaceful manner (verse 31).

Many other Heroes of Faith

"And what more shall I say? For time will fail me if I tell of Gideon, Barak, Samson, Jephthah, of David and Samuel and the prophets. Through faith they conquered kingdoms, administered justice,gained what was promised,shut the mouths of lions, quenched raging fire, escaped the edge of the sword, gained strength in weakness,became mighty in battle, put foreign armies to flight,"

– Hebrews 11:32-34 (NET)

Among the other champions of faith, there were individuals like Gideon, Barak, Samson, and Jephthah, as well as David, Samuel, and the prophets. Through their faith, they conquered kingdoms, practiced righteousness, received promises, silenced lions, extinguished raging fires, escaped deadly threats, gained strength in times of weakness, displayed valor in battle, and routed the armies of foreign invaders (verses 32-34).

"Women received their loved ones back again from death. But others were tortured, refusing to turn from God in order to be set free. They placed their hope in a better life after the resurrection. Some were jeered at, and their backs were cut open with whips. Others were chained in prisons. Some died by stoning, some were sawed in half, and others were killed with the sword. Some went about wearing skins of sheep and goats, destitute and oppressed and mistreated. They were too good for this world, wandering over deserts and mountains, hiding in caves and holes in the ground.

All these people earned a good reputation because of their faith, yet none of them received all that God had promised."

— Hebrews 11:35-39 (NLT)

Women witnessed their loved ones being raised from the dead. Some endured torture, refusing release in order to secure a superior resurrection. Others faced mockery, floggings, chains, and imprisonment. They were stoned, sawn in two, tempted, and killed by the sword. They roamed in sheepskins and goatskins, enduring deprivation, suffering, and torment. The world was unworthy of them as they wandered in deserts, mountains, dens, and caves. All of these individuals, through their faith, received a commendable testimony but did not see the fulfillment of the promise (verses 35-39).

"All these people died still believing what God had promised them. They did not receive what was promised, but they saw it all from a distance and welcomed it. They agreed that they were foreigners and nomads here on earth."

— Hebrews 11:13 (NLT)

All of these individuals passed away in faith, not having realized the promises in their lifetimes. Instead, they saw the promises from a distance, were certain of their fulfillment, welcomed them, and openly acknowledged that they were merely temporary residents and travelers on the earth (verse 13).

"And it is impossible to please God without faith. Anyone who wants to come to him must believe that God exists and that he rewards those who sincerely seek him."

— Hebrews 11:6 (NLT)

Pleasing God is unattainable without faith, because those who approach God must have faith in His existence and in His willingness to reward those who earnestly seek Him (verse 6).

> "Therefore, since we are surrounded by such a huge crowd of witnesses to the life of faith, let us strip off every weight that slows us down, especially the sin that so easily trips us up. And let us run with endurance the race God has set before us. We do this by keeping our eyes on Jesus, the champion who initiates and perfects our faith. Because of the joy awaiting him, he endured the cross, disregarding its shame. Now he is seated in the place of honor beside God's throne."
>
> – Hebrews 12:1-2 (NLT)

So, considering that we are surrounded by such a large group of witnesses, let us get rid of every burden and the sin that clings so closely, and let us run with endurance the race that is set before us. Hebrews 12:1-2 encourages us to keep our focus on Jesus, the One who started and and One who will finish our faith. For the joy set before Him, He endured the cross, disregarding its shame, and now He sits at the right hand of God's throne.

Justification by Faith

> "Therefore, since we have been justified by faith, we have peace with God through our Lord Jesus Christ. Through him we have also obtained access by faith into this grace in which we stand, and we rejoice in hope of the glory of God."
>
> – Romans 5:1-2 (ESV)

Romans 5:1-2 tells us that our faith in Jesus justifies us and brings peace with God. This faith grants us access to God's grace, which we can stand in confidently. We also find joy and hope in the prospect of sharing in God's glory. These verses encourage us to keep our faith strong and trust in the promises ahead.

> "Knowing that a man is not justified by the works of the law, but by the faith of Jesus Christ, even we have believed in Jesus Christ, that we might be justified by the faith of Christ, and not by the works of the law: for by the works of the law shall no flesh be justified."
>
> – Galatians 2:16 (ESV)

We can't be made right with God by following rules and laws, but rather through our faith in Jesus Christ. Galatians 2:16 emphasizes that believing in Him is what justifies us, not trying to be perfect under the law. This verse reminds us that no one can earn their way to righteousness by obeying the law; it's our trust in Christ that makes us right with God.

Purification by Faith

> "God, who knows the heart, showed that he accepted them by giving the Holy Spirit to them, just as he did to us. He did not discriminate between us and them, for he purified their hearts by faith."
>
> – Acts 15:8-9 (NIV)

In Acts 15:8-9, it's evident that God, who truly understands our hearts, recognizes the sincerity of people by granting them the Holy Spirit, just as He does for us. He doesn't differentiate between us and them. Instead, He purifies our hearts through faith. This passage highlights that God values faith and purity of heart above all else, showing that all who believe in Him can receive His grace and blessings.

Sanctification by Faith

"I will rescue you from your own people and from the Gentiles. I am sending you to them to open their eyes and turn them from darkness to light, and from the power of Satan to God, so that they may receive forgiveness of sins and a place among those who are sanctified by faith in me."

— Acts 26:17-18 (NIV)

In Acts 26:17-18, God was speaking to the Apostle Paul. These verses recount a conversation between Paul and Jesus on the road to Damascus, where Jesus called Paul to be His messenger to both the Jewish people and the Gentiles.

God promised to rescue Paul from the people and from the non-Jews to whom He was sending him. His mission was to help them see the truth, to guide them from ignorance to understanding, and to free them from Satan's control so they could embrace God. Because of this, they would receive forgiveness for their sins and share in the inheritance of those who were sanctified or "set apart" by their faith in Him.

Why share our Faith?

There are at least seven compelling reasons for sharing our faith in Christ with those who have not experienced new life in Him.

1. Because God has commanded us to do so:

The final words of Jesus before His ascension to heaven, as well as His command to His disciples, are clearly outlined in the Bible.

"Therefore go and make disciples of all nations, baptizing them in the name of the Father and the Son and
the Holy Spirit, teaching them to obey everything I
have commanded you. And remember, I am with you
always, to the end of the age."

– Matthew 28:19-20 (NET)

In Matthew 28:19-20, Jesus gave His followers a special
mission. He instructed them to go out to all the nations and
make disciples, baptizing them in the name of the Father, the
Son, and the Holy Spirit. They were to teach them to follow
everything Jesus taught. He reminded His followers that He
would always be with them, right to the very end of time.

These words encourage us to share the message of faith
and guide others on their spiritual journey, knowing that Jesus
is always by our side.

"But you will receive power when the Holy Spirit has
come upon you, and you will be my witnesses in Jerusalem, and in all Judea and Samaria, and to the farthest
parts of the earth."

– Acts 1:8 (NET)

Jesus promised his followers in Acts 1:8 that they would
receive power from the Holy Spirit. He told them that with
this power, they would become witnesses for Him, starting in
Jerusalem and spreading to Judea, Samaria, and all the way to
the ends of the earth. This verse serves as a reminder of the
empowerment and mission that comes from the Holy Spirit,
urging us to share the message of faith with the world.

2. Because it demonstrates our love for God:

Christ said that if we truly loved Him we would keep His commandments. We can read this in John 14:15.

"If you love me, keep my commands."

– John 14:15 (NIV)

He said to them, "Go into all the world and preach the gospel to all creation. Whoever believes and is baptized will be saved, but whoever does not believe will be condemned."

– Mark 16:15-16 (NIV)

Jesus gave his disciples a significant task in Mark 16:15-16, urging them to share the Gospel with people all around the world. He emphasized that those who believe and are baptized will experience salvation, while those who do not believe will face condemnation. This message underscores the vital mission of spreading faith and the promise of salvation to everyone.

3. Because all are lost:

As the Scriptures say,"No one is righteous—not even one."

– Romans 3:10 (NLT)

According to Romans 3:10, no one is inherently righteous or perfect. All people have their imperfections and flaws.

"For everyone has sinned; we all fall short of God's glorious standard."

– Romans 3:23 (NLT)

The message of Romans 3:23 is clear: Every person, without exception, has made mistakes and falls short of the perfect standards set by God.

4. Because our sharing is God's chosen method to convey His message to all people.

He could have used angels, but He didn't. Only redeemed sinners can tell lost sinners about Christ.

> "But how can they call on him to save them unless they believe in him? And how can they believe in him if they have never heard about him? And how can they hear about him unless someone tells them?And how will anyone go and tell them without being sent? That is why the Scriptures say, "How beautiful are the feet of messengers who bring good news!"

> But not everyone welcomes the Good News, for Isaiah the prophet said, "Lord, who has believed our message?" So faith comes from hearing, that is, hearing the Good News about Christ.

> – Romans 10:14-17 (NLT)

It's like a chain reaction in Romans 10:14-17: first, people can't call on God if they don't believe in Him, and they can't believe unless they've heard about Him. But they can't hear unless someone shares the message with them. And those who share the message need to be sent for that purpose. The verses even mention how beautiful it is when people bring the good news of peace and glad tidings. But, not everyone has obeyed this message, and it's like a question asked years before by Isaiah, "Who really believes it?"

So, in the end, it emphasizes that faith comes from hearing and hearing from the word of God, emphasizing the power of spreading the gospel.

> "But the believers who were scattered preached the Good News about Jesus wherever they went.Philip, for example, went to the city of Samaria and told the people there about the Messiah."
>
> — Acts 8:4-5 (NLT)

In Acts 8:4-5, it's inspiring to see how those who were scattered went out to various places to share the Word of God. Philip, for instance, went to the city of Samaria and preached about Christ to the people there. This passage reflects the early Christians' zeal to spread the message of faith, even in the face of challenges and adversity, demonstrating the powerful impact of their actions in bringing the gospel to new places and hearts.

5. Because God desires to save all people:

> "There is salvation in no one else! God has given no other name under heaven by which we must be saved."
>
> — Acts 4:12 (NLT)

There is no salvation found in any other name than that of Jesus. Acts 4:12 underscores the uniqueness and significance of His name as the only means by which humanity can find salvation. This verse serves as a cornerstone of Christian faith, emphasizing the central role of Jesus Christ in the redemption and salvation of believers.

> "The Lord isn't really being slow about his promise, as some people think. No, he is being patient for your

sake. He does not want anyone to be destroyed, but wants everyone to repent."

– 2 Peter 3:9 (NLT)

In 2 Peter 3:9, we are reminded that the Lord is patient and not slow to fulfill His promises, contrary to what some may think. His patience is a sign of His desire for all to have the opportunity to turn from their ways and find repentance. This verse reflects God's compassionate and merciful nature, emphasizing His hope that everyone would have the chance to experience true repentance and salvation.

"This is good and pleases God our Savior, who wants everyone to be saved and to understand the truth."

– 1 Timothy 2:3-4 (NLT)

The message in 1 Timothy 2:3-4 is clear and comforting. It tells us that God, our Savior, finds it good and pleasing when people seek salvation and come to understand the truth. His desire is for all humanity to be saved and to come to the knowledge of the truth. This verse reminds us of God's boundless love and His earnest wish for everyone to find the path to salvation and knowledge of His ways.

6. Because someone once shared his faith with us:

It might have been a faithful Bible teacher, a godly Pastor, or a praying parent. They have every right to hope that we will do for others what they did for us.

"Let me now remind you, dear brothers and sisters, of the Good News I preached to you before. You welcomed it then, and you still stand firm in it. It is this Good News that saves you if you continue to believe the message I told you—unless, of course, you believed something that was never true in the first place.

I passed on to you what was most important and what had also been passed on to me. Christ died for our sins, just as the Scriptures said. He was buried, and he was raised from the dead on the third day, just as the Scriptures said."

— 1 Corinthians 15:1-4 (NLT)

1 Corinthians 15:1-4 is a key passage in which Paul outlined the gospel he preached to the Corinthians. He emphasized the importance of holding firmly to the teachings he delivered; specifically the death, burial, and resurrection of Christ as foundational elements of the Christian faith.

7. Because Jesus is coming soon:

The Lord will come as a thief in the night.

"For you know quite well that the day of the Lord's return will come unexpectedly, like a thief in the night. When people are saying, "Everything is peaceful and secure," then disaster will fall on them as suddenly as a pregnant woman's labor pains begin. And there will be no escape."

The Lord will come unexpectedly as a thief in the night, as described in 1 Thessalonians 5:2-3. While people are saying, "Peace and safety," sudden destruction will come upon them, as labor pains on a pregnant woman, and they will not escape. This passage is typically interpreted to mean that the Day of the Lord will arrive without warning, emphasizing the need for vigilance and preparedness among believers.

— 1 Thessalonians 5:2-3 (NLT)

"For as the lightning flashes in the east and shines to the west, so it will be when the Son of Man comes."

– Matthew 24:27 (NLT)

Matthew 24:27 focuses on the nature of Christ's Second Coming. Jesus describes His return as being visible and unmistakable, likening it to lightning that flashes across the sky, visible from east to west. This picture conveys the suddenness and clarity with which Christ's return will be recognized, unlike any secret or hidden event.

"However, no one knows the day or hour when these things will happen, not even the angels in heaven or the Son himself.Only the Father knows."

– Matthew 24:36 (NLT)

There is uncertainty about the timing of the Lord's return. Jesus states in Matthew 24:36 that no one knows about that day or hour, not even the angels in heaven, nor the Son, but only the Father. This passage is often cited to caution against predicting the exact time of the end times, emphasizing that it is known only to God.

What is to be shared?

Before discussing what we should share about our faith, let's remember what we should avoid. We must not confuse the unbelieving world by making them believe that church membership, tithing, offering, or any good works are connected to becoming a Christian.

"For it is by grace you have been saved, through faith— and this is not from yourselves, it is the gift of God— not by works, so that no one can boast."

– Ephesians 2:8-9 (NLT)

Ephesians 2:8-9 explains that people are saved by God's grace through their faith. This is not something they can earn by themselves; it's a gift from God. It's not the result of any good actions, so no one can boast about it. Basically, it means that salvation is freely given by God and not something we can achieve on our own.

> "He has saved us and called us to a holy life—not because of anything we have done but because of his own purpose and grace. This grace was given us in Christ Jesus before the beginning of time,"
>
> – 2 Timothy 1:9 (NIV)

God saves people and calls them to live a holy life, not because of anything they've done, but because of His own plan and kindness. 2 Timothy 1:9 explains that his kindness was given through Jesus Christ long ago, even before time started. It means that God's decision to save people is based on His purpose and grace, not on their deeds, and this plan has been in place since before the beginning of time.

Actually, we have but one thing to share with the unsaved, and that is the gospel of Christ. According to Paul, it involves the death and resurrection of Christ.

God's *Word says all are sinners, condemned to hell.*

> "All we like sheep have gone astray; we have turned—every one—to his own way; and the Lord has laid on him the iniquity of us all."
>
> – Isaiah 53:6 (ESV)

Isaiah 53:6 explains that everyone has strayed away from God, like sheep wandering off. Everyone has turned to their own way, doing what they think is right, rather than what God wants. But, God has laid on Jesus the sins of everyone. It implies that Jesus bears the consequences of everyone's wrong-doings.

> "but God shows his love for us in that while we were still sinners, Christ died for us."
>
> — Romans 5:8 (ESV)

How does God demonstrate His love for us? Romans 5:8 explains that even though people were still sinners, Christ died for them. God's love is so great that He sent Jesus to die for people's sins, even before they turned away from their sins.

> "Therefore, just as sin came into the world through one man, and death through sin, and so death spread to all men because all sinned"
>
> — Romans 5:12 (ESV)

According to Romans 5:12, sin entered the world through one man, and death came because of sin. So, death spread to everyone because everyone sinned. This 'one man' refers to Adam, and it suggests that his actions brought sin and death into the world, affecting all humanity.

> "For as by a man came death, by a man has come also the resurrection of the dead."
>
> — 1 Corinthians 15:21 (ESV)

Since death came through a man, the resurrection of the dead also comes through a man. 1 Corinthians 15:21 is referring to Jesus Christ, indicating that just as death came into the world through Adam, the promise of resurrection and life comes through Christ.

> "And if anyone's name was not found written in the book of life, he was thrown into the lake of fire."
>
> – Revelation 20:15 (ESV)

Revelation 20:15 tells us that anyone whose name is not found written in the Book of Life will be thrown into the lake of fire. This is part of a vision of judgment, explaining that those not recorded in the Book of Life, which represents those who have not accepted Jesus Christ as Savior, face eternal punishment.

There is nothing a lost person can do on his own to save himself.

> "We are all like one who is unclean, all our so-called righteous acts are like a menstrual rag in your sight. We all wither like a leaf; our sins carry us away like the wind."
>
> – Isaiah 64:6 (NET)

Isaiah 64:6 describes how all human good deeds are like dirty rags in God's sight. It suggests that people are unclean because of their sins, and even their attempts at doing good are not enough to make them pure. Humans can't achieve righteousness or purity on their own. We all need God's intervention.

> "Evil people self-destruct; those who hate the godly are punished."
>
> – Psalm 34:21 (NET)

Evil will cause the downfall of the wicked. Psalm 34:21 says that those who do wrong will be killed by their own evil deeds. This verse is about the natural consequences of evil actions and implies that those who do harm will ultimately be harmed themselves.

> "He will pay them back for their sin. He will destroy them because of their evil; the LORD our God will destroy them."
>
> – Psalm 94:23 (NET)

God will bring back the wickedness of evil people upon themselves. God will destroy them for their sins. Psalm 94:23 emphasizes that God is just and will ensure that evil people receive punishment for their wrongdoing.

Christ was born, crucified, and resurrected to save lost people from their sin.

> "For this is how God loved the world: He gave his one and only Son, so that everyone who believes in him will not perish but have eternal life."
>
> – John 3:16 (NLT)

The famous verse, John 3:16, states that God loved the world so much that He gave His only Son, so that everyone who believes in Him won't perish but will have eternal life. It emphasizes God's love for all people and the promise of eternal life through belief in Jesus.

> "This is a trustworthy saying, and everyone should accept it: "Christ Jesus came into the world to save sinners"—and I am the worst of them all."
>
> – 1 Timothy 1:15 (NLT)

Christ Jesus came into the world to save sinners. 1 Timothy 1:15 highlights the purpose of Jesus' coming to earth, which was to offer salvation to sinners, acknowledging that everyone is in need of this salvation.

> "But he was pierced for our rebellion, crushed for our sins. He was beaten so we could be whole. He was whipped so we could be healed."
>
> – Isaiah 53:5 (NLT)

In the Old Testament, Isaiah prophesies about Jesus. Chapter 53, verse 5 says that He was wounded for our transgressions and crushed for our iniquities. The punishment that brought us peace was on Him, and by His wounds, we are healed. This verse speaks of the suffering of Jesus and how it was meant to heal and save humanity from sin.

> "He was handed over to die because of our sins, and he was raised to life to make us right with God."
>
> – Romans 4:25 (NLT)

Jesus was delivered over to death for our sins and was raised to life for our justification. Romans 4:25 connects Jesus' death and resurrection to the forgiveness of sins and the justification (being made right with God) of believers.

> "He personally carried our sins in his body on the cross so that we can be dead to sin and live for what is right. By his wounds you are healed."
>
> – 1 Peter 2:24 (NLT)

1 Peter 2:24 states that Jesus Himself bore our sins in His body on the cross, so that we might die to sins and live for righteousness. By his wounds, we have been healed. This verse

emphasizes that Jesus' sacrifice on the cross was to take away our sins and to enable us to live a life of righteousness.

To be saved, a sinner must believe God's Word and invite Christ into his heart by faith.

> "Very truly I tell you, whoever hears my word and believes him who sent me has eternal life and will not be judged but has crossed over from death to life."
>
> — John 5:24 (NIV)

In John 5:24 Jesus says that anyone who hears His word and believes in God, who sent Him, has eternal life. They will not be judged but have already crossed over from death to life. This emphasizes the importance of believing in Jesus' teachings and in God to gain eternal life and avoid judgment.

> "Whoever believes in him is not condemned, but whoever does not believe stands condemned already because they have not believed in the name of God's one and only Son"
>
> — John 3:18 (NIV)

Whoever believes in Jesus is not condemned, but whoever does not believe stands condemned already because they have not believed in the name of God's one and only Son. John 3:18 highlights the distinction between those who believe in Jesus and those who do not, with belief being the key to avoiding condemnation.

> They replied, "Believe in the Lord Jesus, and you will be saved—you and your household."
>
> — Acts 16:31 (NIV)

The Apostle Paul told a jailer to believe in the Lord Jesus, and he and his household would be saved. This simple statement in Acts 16:31 underscores the necessity of faith in Jesus for salvation, implying that this belief extends to the believer's family as well.

> "Very truly I tell you, the one who believes has eternal life. I am the bread of life."
>
> — John 6:47-48 (NIV)

In John 6:47-48, Jesus compared Himself to the bread of life, indicating that belief in Him is essential for eternal life, much like bread is necessary for physical life.

How to share our Faith?

> "And they went out and preached everywhere, while the Lord worked with them and confirmed the message by accompanying signs."
>
> — Mark 16:20 (ESV)

Mark 16:20 describes how the disciples went out and preached everywhere, while the Lord worked with them and confirmed the message by accompanying signs. It emphasizes the early Christians' active role in spreading Jesus' teachings and the divine support they received through miraculous signs.

> "while God also bore witness by signs and wonders and various miracles and by gifts of the Holy Spirit distributed according to his will."
>
> — Hebrews 2:4 (ESV)

The message of salvation was confirmed by God with signs, wonders, various miracles, and gifts of the Holy Spirit were distributed according to His will. We see this in Hebrews 2:4.

"Men of Israel, hear these words: Jesus of Nazareth, a man attested to you by God with mighty works and wonders and signs that God did through him in your midst, as you yourselves know"

– Acts 2:22 (ESV)

Peter spoke about Jesus in Acts 2:22, describing Him as a man accredited by God to the people through miracles, wonders, and signs, which God did among them through His Son. Jesus showed us by example how we can share our faith and have our words validated by heaven.

Rules to share the Faith

In order to share our faith successfully, we must keep the following rules in our minds.

First, we must be clean vessels. God reminds Isaiah the prophet of this in 52:11. This verse calls for the people of Israel to depart from Babylon and to purify themselves, especially those who carried the vessels of the Lord. It emphasizes the need for cleanliness and holiness among those who serve God.

"Depart, depart, go out from there! Touch no unclean thing! Come out from it and be pure, you who carry the articles of the Lord's house."

– Isaiah 52:11 (NIV)

"Tell Aaron and his sons to treat with respect the sacred offerings the Israelites consecrate to me, so they will not profane my holy name. I am the Lord."

– Leviticus 22:2 (NIV)

The importance of treating what is dedicated to God with reverence is underscored in Leviticus 22:2. God commanded

Moses to tell the sons of Aaron to treat the holy offerings of the Israelites with respect so they would not profane God's holy name.

While God does not demand golden or silver vessels, He does require clean ones. King David prayed for forgiveness and cleansing after committing adultery and murder. In Psalm 51:10-13, he pleaded not to be cast away from God's presence or to have the Holy Spirit taken from him. The king longed for restoration of the joy of salvation and a willing spirit to sustain him. He wanted his example to help teach other sinners about God's ways.

> Create in me a pure heart, O God, and renew a steadfast spirit within me.Do not cast me from your presence or take your Holy Spirit from me. Restore to me the joy of your salvation and grant me a willing spirit, to sustain me. Then I will teach transgressors your ways, so that sinners will turn back to you.
>
> — Psalm 51:10-13 (NIV)

> "Now the Lord is the Spirit, and where the Spirit of the Lord is, there is freedom."
>
> — 2 Corinthians 3:17 (NIV)

Where the Spirit of the Lord is, there is freedom. 2 Corinthians 3:17 tells us that the presence of God's Spirit brings liberty and transformation in the lives of believers.

We must be able to clearly give the simple facts of the gospel without going into profound theological concepts. Philip, the evangelist, demonstrated how to do this when he dealt with a traveler in the desert. In Acts 8:34-45, the Ethiopian eunuch, reading a passage from Isaiah, asked Philip to explain it to him.

Philip then taught that the Scripture he was reading is about Jesus, and he shared the good news about Jesus with him. This shows the importance of understanding Scripture in the context of Jesus' life and mission.

> The eunuch asked Philip, "Tell me, was the prophet talking about himself or someone else?" So beginning with this same Scripture, Philip told him the Good News about Jesus.
>
> – Acts 8:34-35 (NLT)

> Then he said, "When I was with you before, I told you that everything written about me in the law of Moses and the prophets and in the Psalms must be fulfilled." Then he opened their minds to understand the Scriptures. And he said, "Yes, it was written long ago that the Messiah would suffer and die and rise from the dead on the third day. It was also written that this message would be proclaimed in the authority of his name to all the nations, beginning in Jerusalem: 'There is forgiveness of sins for all who repent.' You are witnesses of all these things.
>
> – Luke 24:44-48 (NLT)

In Luke 24:44-48, Jesus explained to His disciples that everything written about Him in the Law of Moses, the Prophets, and the Psalms must be fulfilled. He opened their minds to understand the Scriptures, stating that repentance for the forgiveness of sins will be preached in His name to all nations.

We must avoid arguments and stick to the basic issues of man's sin and Christ's blood. Often, unbelievers will attempt to sidestep the gospel by asking unrelated questions, such as "Where did Cain get his wife?"

> Then someone called from the crowd, "Teacher, please tell my brother to divide our father's estate with me."
>
> Jesus replied, "Friend, who made me a judge over you to decide such things as that?" Then he said, "Beware! Guard against every kind of greed. Life is not measured by how much you own."
>
> – Luke 12:13-15 (NLT)

Jesus dealt with this kind of situation in Luke 12:13-15. When someone asked Him to settle a family inheritance dispute, Jesus refused, saying that life is not about having a lot of possessions. He told them to be on guard against all kinds of greed.

We must use the Word of God. Paul's tremendous success as an evangelist can be linked directly to his constant use of God's Word.

> "As was Paul's custom, he went to the synagogue service, and for three Sabbaths in a row he used the Scriptures to reason with the people. He explained the prophecies and proved that the Messiah must suffer and rise from the dead. He said, "This Jesus I'm telling you about is the Messiah."
>
> – Acts 17:2-3 (NLT)

As was his custom, Paul went into a synagogue and for three Sabbath days he reasoned with them from the Scriptures, explaining and proving that the Messiah had to suffer and rise from the dead, and that Jesus is the Messiah. (Acts 17:2-3)

> "He refuted the Jews with powerful arguments in public debate. Using the Scriptures, he explained to them that Jesus was the Messiah."
>
> – Acts 18:28 (NLT)

Apollos, one of Paul's co-workers, vigorously refuted the Jews in public debate in Acts 18:28, showing from the Scriptures that Jesus was the Messiah.

"Remind everyone about these things, and command them in God's presence to stop fighting over words. Such arguments are useless, and they can ruin those who hear them. Work hard so you can present yourself to God and receive his approval. Be a good worker, one who does not need to be ashamed and who correctly explains the word of truth."

– 2 Timothy 2:14-15 (NLT)

"But as for you, continue in what you have learned and have firmly believed, knowing from whom you learned it and how from childhood you have been acquainted with the sacred writings, which are able to make you wise for salvation through faith in Christ Jesus."

– 2 Timothy 3:14-15 (ESV)

"All Scripture is breathed out by God and profitable for teaching, for reproof, for correction, and for training in righteousness"

– 2 Timothy 3:14-16 (ESV)

Paul advised Timothy to remind people of certain truths, warning against quarreling about words. In 2 Timothy 2:14-15 and 3:14-17, He encouraged the young pastor to present himself to God as one approved, a worker who does not need to be ashamed and who correctly handles the word of truth. Paul admonished Timothy to continue in what he had learned, knowing from whom he learned it. He reminded him of the importance of Scripture, which is God-breathed and useful for teaching, rebuking, correcting, and training in righteousness.

We must depend upon the Spirit of God.

> "But they could not withstand the wisdom and the Spirit with which he was speaking."
>
> — Acts 6:10 (ESV)

Those who argued with Stephen in Acts 6:10 could not stand up against the wisdom and the Spirit by which he spoke. The Holy Spirit gives power of spiritual wisdom in discussions and debates.

> "These things I have spoken to you while I am still with you. 26 But the Helper, the Holy Spirit, whom the Father will send in my name, he will teach you all things and bring to your remembrance all that I have said to you."
>
> — John 14:25-26 (ESV)

> "But you will receive power when the Holy Spirit has come upon you, and you will be my witnesses in Jerusalem and in all Judea and Samaria, and to the end of the earth."
>
> — Acts 1:8 (ESV)

Jesus told His disciples that the Holy Spirit, whom the Father would send in His name, would teach them all things and remind them of everything He had said to them. (John 14:25-26) Then in Acts 1:8, Jesus told His disciples that they would receive power when the Holy Spirit came upon them and they would be His witnesses in Jerusalem, and in all Judea and Samaria, and to the ends of the earth. Jesus emphasized the empowering role of the Holy Spirit in the spread of the gospel.

"And when they had set them in the midst, they in-
quired, "By what power or by what name did you do
this?" Then Peter, filled with the Holy Spirit, said to
them, "Rulers of the people and elders,

– Acts 4:7-8 (ESV)

Acts 4:7-8 tells us that Peter, filled with the Holy Spirit,
spoke to the religious leaders with confidence about the healing of a lame man in the name of Jesus Christ. This demonstrates the boldness and power given by the Holy Spirit in proclaiming the message of Jesus.

When should we share our Faith?

The question of when to share our faith is closely connected to when a sinner should accept Christ. The Bible is clear:
God's accepted time is today. The reason for this is simple—a
sinner has no assurance that they will live to see tomorrow.
Therefore, we are called to witness at any time, all the time, in
any place, and everywhere.

The Apostle Paul showed us how this should be done. He
witnessed everywhere, including a prison at midnight (Acts
16:25-31), and even on a sinking ship during a dark and stormy
day (Acts 27:20-25).

In Acts 8:26-39, we read how an Angel of the Lord spoke
to Philip, saying, "Arise and go toward the south along the road
which goes down from Jerusalem to Gaza." This is a desert.
So Philip arose and went. A man of authority from Ethiopia,
returning from Jerusalem after worship, was sitting in his chariot, reading Isaiah, the Prophet. Philip helped him understand
the passage he was reading, and beginning at this Scripture,
preached Jesus to him. When the eunuch, having believed that

Jesus is the Son of God, saw water nearby on the way, he came down from the chariot. Both Philip and the eunuch went down into the water, and Philip baptized him.

A famous evangelist once ended a revival meeting in Chicago by advising the unbelievers who were present to go home and seriously consider the claims of the gospel. He urged them to return the following night, prepared to make a decision for Christ. However, on that very night, October 8, 1871, the devastating Chicago fire erupted. It ravaged nearly four miles of buildings and claimed 250 lives. The evangelist then vowed never to end a service without giving an immediate invitation to accept Christ.

> "Don't brag about tomorrow, since you don't know what the day will bring."
>
> – Proverbs 27:1 (NLT)

We are not to boast about tomorrow, as no one knows what a day may bring. Proverbs 27:1 emphasizes the uncertainty of the future and cautions against arrogance or overconfidence in one's plans.

> "Look here, you who say, "Today or tomorrow we are going to a certain town and will stay there a year. We will do business there and make a profit." How do you know what your life will be like tomorrow? Your life is like the morning fog—it's here a little while, then it's gone. What you ought to say is, "If the Lord wants us to, we will live and do this or that." Otherwise you are boasting about your own pretentious plans, and all such boasting is evil."
>
> – James 4:13-16 (NLT)

James 4:13-16 warns against arrogance in planning for the future. He criticizes those who make confident plans about business and profit without considering God's will, reminding them that life is like a mist that appears for a while and then vanishes. He concludes that boasting about such plans is evil.

> "And I'll sit back and say to myself, My friend, you have enough stored away for years to come. Now take it easy! Eat, drink, and be merry! But God said to him, 'You fool! You will die this very night. Then who will get everything you worked for?"
>
> – Luke 12:19-20 (NLT)

Jesus told a parable in Luke 12:19-20 of a rich man who stored up many goods and planned to relax and enjoy life. God called the man a fool, telling him that he would die that night, and asked who would get what he had prepared for himself. This parable warns against placing security in material wealth and ignoring God.

> Be careful then, dear brothers and sisters. Make sure that your own hearts are not evil and unbelieving, turning you away from the living God. You must warn each other every day, while it is still "today," so that none of you will be deceived by sin and hardened against God.
>
> – Hebrews 3:12-13 (NLT)

We are cautioned in Hebrews 3:12-13 against having sinful, unbelieving hearts that turn away from the living God. This passage urges believers to encourage one another daily, as long as it is called "Today," so that none may be hardened by the deceitfulness of sin.

Remember what it says: "Today when you hear his voice, don't harden your hearts as Israel did when they rebelled."

– Hebrews 3:15 (NLT)

So God set another time for entering his rest, and that time is today. God announced this through David much later in the words already quoted: "Today when you hear his voice, don't harden your hearts."

– Hebrews 4:7 (NLT)

Both Hebrews 3:15 and 4:7 reiterate the importance of responding to God's voice "today."

For God says,"At just the right time, I heard you.On the day of salvation, I helped you." Indeed, the "right time" is now. Today is the day of salvation.

– 2 Corinthians 6:2 (NLT)

Paul quoted a scripture in 2 Corinthians 6:2 saying that at the right time, God listened and on the day of salvation, He helped. Paul emphasized that "now is the time of God's favor, now is the day of salvation."

Walking in the Spirit

Confession

An important prerequisite to walking in the Spirit is the confession of sin. Sin must be confessed in order to restore fellowship and to continue receiving God's power. Confession means that we agree with God about our sin. This involves much more than simply acknowledging the sin. Confession requires an attitude of sorrow for the sin and a willingness to turn from it. It does not mean that we will never commit the same sin again, but it does mean that the attitude of repent-ance is present.

> This is the message we have heard from him and de-clare to you: God is light; in him there is no darkness at all. If we claim to have fellowship with him and yet walk in the darkness, we lie and do not live out the truth. But if we walk in the light, as he is in the light, we have fellowship with one another, and the blood of Jesus, his Son, purifies us from all sin.If we claim to be without sin, we deceive ourselves and the truth is not in us. If we confess our sins, he is faithful and just and will forgive us our sins and purify us from all unright-eousness. If we claim we have not sinned, we make him out to be a liar and his word is not in us.
>
> – 1 John 1:5-10 (NIV)

1 John 1:5-10 discusses walking in the light of God. It ex-plains that God is light and in Him, there is no darkness. If we claim to have fellowship with Him but walk in darkness, we lie and do not live out the truth. Confessing our sins is essential, as God is faithful to forgive and purify us from all unrighteous-ness.

Confession should be made at the moment the Christian becomes aware of sin. Additionally, the Scriptures specify two particular times for confession: before the close of the day and before the Lord's Supper is observed. Failure to do this is a special cause for discipline from the Lord.

> "In your anger do not sin": Do not let the sun go down while you are still angry"
>
> – Ephesians 4:26 (NIV)

Ephesians 4:26 advises us not to sin in anger. "It says, in your anger do not sin." Do not let the sun go down while you are still angry. It emphasizes the need to manage anger responsibly.

> "Therefore, whoever eats the bread or drinks the cup of the Lord in an unworthy manner will be guilty of sinning against the body and blood of the Lord. A person ought to examine themselves before they eat of the bread and drink from the cup. For those who eat and drink without discerning the body of Christ eat and drink judgment on themselves. That is why many among you are weak and sick, and a number of you have fallen asleep."
>
> – 1 Corinthians 11:27-30 (NIV)

Paul warns about taking the Lord's Supper (Communion) in an unworthy manner. In 1 Corinthians 11:27-30, he explains that those who eat and drink without discerning the body of Christ eat and drink judgment on themselves.

Yielding

Confessing sin alone isn't enough to automatically enable a believer to walk in the Spirit. He must then become a yielded instrument for God's service. This yielding involves offering oneself entirely, both body and mind, because actions are conceived in the mind and are executed through the body. In other words, what the mind conceives, the body carries out. Therefore, a person's entire being must be presented to God's service through a decisive act of the will. Yielding shouldn't be limited to a willingness to perform specific tasks. Rather, the dedicated person does whatever God commands.

"and do not present your members to sin as instruments to be used for unrighteousness, but present yourselves to God as those who are alive from the dead and your members to God as instruments to be used for righteousness."

— Romans 6:13 (NET)

Romans 6:13 encourages believers not to offer any part of themselves to sin as an instrument of wickedness, but rather to offer themselves to God and their parts as instruments of righteousness.

"Therefore I exhort you, brothers and sisters, by the mercies of God, to present your bodies as a sacrifice—alive, holy, and pleasing to God—which is your reasonable service."

— Romans 12:1 (NET)

The teaching found in Romans 12:1-2 urges believers to offer their bodies as living sacrifices, holy and pleasing to God, and not to conform to the pattern of this world but be transformed by the renewing of their minds.

"For you were bought at a price. Therefore glorify God with your body."

— 1 Corinthians 6:20 (NET)

Believers are reminded in 1 Corinthians 6:20 that we are extremely valuable to God. We were bought at a price and therefore should honor God with our bodies and in our spirits.

Yielding can lead not only to dedication but also to separation.

Since the world is resolutely opposed to God, one cannot revel or indulge in its lusts, and at the same time, do the will of

God. Therefore, the concept of separation involves an "unfashionable" demeanor in terms of spirit, thought, values, and actions when measured against the world's standards.

> By forsaking the right path they have gone astray, because they followed the way of Balaam son of Bosor, who loved the wages of unrighteousness, yet was rebuked for his own transgression (a dumb donkey,-speaking with a human voice,restrained the prophet's madness). These men are waterless springs and mists driven by a storm, for whom the utter depths of darkness have been reserved.
>
> – 2 Peter 2:15-17 (NET)

Peter warned against false teachers, comparing them to Balaam, who was rebuked for his wrongdoing. In 2 Peter 2:15-17, he described these teachers as springs without water and mists driven by a storm.

> "Therefore, get your minds ready for action by being fully sober, and set your hope completely on the grace that will be brought to you when Jesus Christ is revealed.Like obedient children, do not comply with[d] the evil urges you used to follow in your ignorance,but, like the Holy One who called you, become holy yourselves in all of your conduct,"
>
> – 1 Peter 1:13-15 (NET)

Believers are encouraged to prepare their minds for action, be sober-minded, set their hope fully on the grace to be given when Jesus Christ is revealed, and to be holy in all their conduct (1 Peter 1:13-15).

Finally, yielding includes the transformation of the mind. This work is accomplished through a lifetime of "renewing" the mind. Man's mind has been darkened by sin and must be brought to the place where it thinks as God thinks.

This renewal primarily occurs through prayer to God in all aspects of life and constant meditation on God's word. This transformation is a lifelong process that won't be fully accomplished until we are with Christ. Along life's journey, though, it brings a peace and delight that can only be experienced by embracing the mind of Christ.

> "The mind governed by the flesh is death, but the mind governed by the Spirit is life and peace. The mind governed by the flesh is hostile to God; it does not submit to God's law, nor can it do so. Those who are in the realm of the flesh cannot please God."
>
> – Romans 8:6-8 (NIV)

Romans 8:6-8 explains that the mind governed by the flesh is dead, but the mind governed by the Spirit is filled with life and peace. The mind governed by the flesh is hostile to God and cannot please God.

> "Do not be anxious about anything, but in every situation, by prayer and petition, with thanksgiving, present your requests to God. And the peace of God, which transcends all understanding, will guard your hearts and your minds in Christ Jesus."
>
> – Philippians 4:6-7 (NIV)

Paul advised us in Philippians 4:6-7 not to be anxious about anything, but in every situation, by prayer and petition, with thanksgiving, present our requests to God. The peace of God, which goes beyond our understanding, will guard our hearts and minds in Christ Jesus.

Filling

Being filled with the Spirit means being controlled by the Spirit. This is crucial for successfully living the Christian life. Unlike the indwelling of the Spirit, a believer is filled over and over again. Notice the emphasis on the present tense—"be filled." We find several biblical examples of Christians who were filled more than once.

Equally important, we observe that filling is not an option. It is a command to be obeyed.

> "All of them were filled with the Holy Spirit and began to speak in other tongues as the Spirit enabled them."
>
> — Acts 2:4 (NIV)

We read in Acts 2:4 of the event of Pentecost where the apostles and those praying with them were filled with the Holy Spirit and began to speak in other languages as the Spirit enabled them. It marks the fulfillment of Jesus' promise of the Holy Spirit and the beginning of the Christian church's global mission.

> "After they prayed, the place where they were meeting was shaken. And they were all filled with the Holy Spirit and spoke the word of God boldly."
>
> — Acts 4:31 (NIV)

After the believers prayed, Acts 4:31 says that their meeting place was shaken, and they were all filled with the Holy Spirit and spoke the Word of God boldly.

The next important question is, "How can someone be filled with the Spirit?" The prerequisites are simply confessing sin and yielding to God. Confessing sin means agreeing with God about the person's sin, and yielding primarily involves dedicating oneself to God. As the believer chooses to obey in these areas, he is filled with the Spirit and enabled to manifest Christ-like character. This obedience may be accompanied by prayer.

The certainty of being filled with the Spirit may be confirmed by the believer's faith and life. The believer must, of course, believe God's Word that meeting the conditions will result in that filling. The Spirit-filled individual will exhibit the Christ-like character described in Galatians 5:22-23 as the fruit of the Spirit. Included in that list are all the vibrant, attractive qualities desired by all Christians. It is delightful that any Christian may possess them and be transformed by the filling of the Spirit.

> "Do not get drunk on wine, which leads to debauchery. Instead, be filled with the Spirit, speaking to one another with psalms, hymns, and songs from the Spirit. Sing and make music from your heart to the Lord"
>
> – Ephesians 5:18-19 (NIV)

In Ephesians 5:18-19 Paul advises believers not to get drunk on wine, which leads to debauchery, but to be filled with the Spirit. He suggests speaking to one another with psalms, hymns, and songs from the Spirit, singing and making music from the heart to the Lord.

> "On one occasion, while he was eating with them, he gave them this command: "Do not leave Jerusalem, but wait for the gift my Father promised, which you have heard me speak about. For John baptized with[a] water, but in a few days you will be baptized with the Holy Spirit."
>
> - Acts 1:4-5 (NIV)

Jesus instructed His disciples to wait in Jerusalem for the gift the Father promised, which they heard Him speak about. This account, found in Acts 1:4-5, explained that John had baptized with water, but in a few days, they would be baptized with the Holy Spirit.

Beginning the New Life

By nature, mankind is sinful and needs the righteousness of God. We must be separated from sin and set apart to righteousness.

To approach God, we must do so on His terms. We must possess new lives in which our sins have been forgiven and obliterated.

Understanding the necessity of a new life is one thing, but acquiring it is an entirely different matter. When we are "saved," we are described as new creatures (2 Cor. 5:17); we have passed from death to life (John 5:24); we have moved from the domain of darkness to the kingdom of God's Son (Col. 1:13); we have experienced a new birth (John 3:3); and we have been adopted by God (Gal. 4:4-5). These wonderful results of having a new life in Christ are freely available to all who place their trust in Christ for salvation.

Need for the New Life: Holiness of God

You cannot see or hear God without holiness. Holiness is required to come before God. Adam and Eve, when they heard the voice of the LORD God walking in the garden in the cool of the day, hid themselves from the presence of the LORD God among the trees of the garden. They disobeyed God, lost their holiness, and could not come before the Holy God.

"Not a single person on earth is always good and never sins"

— Ecclesiastes 7:20 (NLT)

Ecclesiastes 7:20 states that there is no righteous person on earth who always does good and never sins.

They were calling out to each other, "Holy, holy, holy is the Lord of Heaven's Armies! The whole earth is filled with his glory!"

— Isaiah 6:3 (NLT)

In a vision recorded in Isaiah 6:3, the prophet saw seraphim (angels) calling to one another, saying, "Holy, holy, holy is the Lord Almighty; the whole earth is full of his glory." This verse emphasizes the absolute holiness of God.

Way to the New Life: New Life

This is a free gift of God. There is nothing that one can do to earn this gift. If one could earn it, it would not be a gift; it would be wages. The gift of God is eternal life. One receives this gift when he believes in Jesus as his personal Savior.

"For the wages of sin is death, but the free gift of God is eternal life through Christ Jesus our Lord."

— Romans 6:23 (NLT)

In Romans 6:23, Paul explained that the payment for sin is death. But because of His great love, God offers us a gift of eternal life, thanks to Jesus Christ our Lord.

They replied, "Believe in the Lord Jesus and you will be saved, along with everyone in your household."

– Acts 16:31 (NLT)

Paul and Silas told their jailer in Acts 16:31 to believe in the Lord Jesus, and they would be saved along with their household.

Results of the New Life: Everlasting Life

The new life in Christ is called the "everlasting (eternal) life." The word "life" stresses the quality of this new personal relationship with God that gives us a fullness of spiritual vitality that we lacked before.

> "I tell you the truth, those who listen to my message and believe in God who sent me have eternal life. They will never be condemned for their sins, but they have already passed from death into life."

– John 5:24 (NLT)

Jesus says in John 5:24 that whoever hears His Word and believes in Him who sent Jesus has eternal life. They will not be judged but they have crossed over from death to life. There is promise of eternal life through belief in Jesus!

> "This means that anyone who belongs to Christ has become a new person. The old life is gone; a new life has begun!"

– 2 Corinthians 5:17 (NLT)

Paul states that anyone in Christ is a new creation; the old has gone, and the new is here. This verse found in 2 Corinthians 5:17 speaks to the life-changing power of faith in Christ.

The Christian is now a new man as opposed to the old man that he was before he became a Christian. He has become a new creation with a renewed nature, undergoing a spiritual transformation within his inner man when he put his faith in Christ as his Savior.

Assurance of the New Life: Promise of God

Often, Christians may doubt their salvation solely because they don't feel saved. They fail to understand that their salvation is based on God's promise rather than their emotional feelings.

"...in hope of eternal life, which God, who never lies, promised before the ages began"

– Titus 1:2 (ESV)

Titus tells us of the hope of eternal life, which God, who does not lie, promised before the beginning of time. It underscores the assurance and ancient origin of this promise.

The fullness of God, the "Holy Trinity" is totally involved in this promise of our salvation:

The promise and work of the Father–The Father has promised to graciously accept all repenting sinners in Christ.

"he predestined us for adoption to himself as sons through Jesus Christ, according to the purpose of his will, 6 to the praise of his glorious grace, with which he has blessed us in the Beloved."

– Ephesians 1:5-6 (ESV)

Paul explains in Ephesians 1:5-6 that through Jesus, believers are predestined for adoption to sonship according to

God's pleasure and will, to the praise of His glorious grace. It highlights the concept of believers being chosen and favored by God.

The promise and work of the Son—The Son has promised eternal and abundant life. Right now, He is praying for us and ministering to us at His Father's right hand.

"The thief comes only to steal and kill and destroy. I came that they may have life and have it abundantly."

– John 10:10 (ESV)

Jesus declared in John 10:10 that He came so that people may have life and have it abundantly. This verse speaks to the full and fulfilling life Jesus offers beyond mere existence.

The promise of the Holy Spirit—The Holy Spirit has promised to indwell the believer, placing all believers into the body of Christ. He assures us of our union with God Himself.

"And I will ask the Father, and he will give you another Helper, to be with you forever, even the Spirit of truth, whom the world cannot receive, because it neither sees him nor knows him. You know him, for he dwells with you and will be in you."

– John 14:16-17 (ESV)

Jesus promised to send the Advocate, the Holy Spirit, who would be with believers forever. The Spirit is described as the Spirit of truth, whom the world cannot understand. It reminds us of the constant presence and guidance of the Holy Spirit in believers' lives.

Growing in the New Life

Knowing how to grow in the new life is essential.

Word of God – Bible Study

This saying remains ever true: "Sin will keep you from God's Word, and God's Word will keep you from sin." Therefore, the primary and most essential step toward growing in the new life is to read and study the Word of God.

Prayer

The second important factor in Christian growth is prayer. Prayer may be defined as talking with and listening to God. We talk to Him with our lips and hearts, and He talks to us through His will and His Word. Prayer involves a two-way conversation. Spiritual maturity is impossible without a systematic prayer life.

Stewardship

God intended that the Christian life should be dynamic, not static. We should sit under the teaching of the Word of God, understand and apply its meaning and implications, and serve God and our fellow believers. The Spirit of God has given us spiritual gifts, but those gifts are worthless unless they are put to use in the service of God and His church.

> "And we have different gifts according to the grace given to us. If the gift is prophecy, that individual must use it in proportion to his faith."
>
> — Romans 12:6 (NET)

In Romans 12:6, Paul spoke about having different gifts according to the grace given to each believer. He encourages the use of these diverse spiritual gifts for the community's benefit.

> "For you were called to freedom, brothers and sisters;only do not use your freedom as an opportunity to indulge your flesh, but through love serve one another."
>
> — Galatians 5:13 (NET)

Paul reminded the Galatians in chapter five, verse thirteen that they were called to be free, but not to use their freedom to indulge the flesh; rather, to serve one another humbly in love.

Worship

Worship is another essential aspect of spiritual growth. It involves showing honor and respect to God, participating in both private and public worship ceremonies, and joyfully serving the Lord as Christians. Those who, in reverence and service, submit to the lordship of Christ will experience spiritual growth. Only God Almighty is worthy of worship.

> "Give to the Lord the glory he deserves! Bring your offering and come into his presence. Worship the Lord in all his holy splendor."
>
> — 1 Chronicles 16:29 (NLT)

1 Chronicles 16:29 calls for giving to the Lord the glory due His name, bringing an offering, and coming before Him in worship. It emphasizes the importance of honoring God with reverence and offerings.

"You are worthy, O Lord our God, to receive glory and honor and power. For you created all things, and they exist because you created what you pleased."

– Revelation 4:11 (NLT)

A vision of heaven described in Revelation 4:11, shows the elders worshiping God, acknowledging that He is worthy to receive glory, honor, and power, for He created all things, and by His will, they exist and were created. The Creator is sovereign and worthy!

Participation in the Local Church

The ultimate reason for our participation in a local church lies in the direct command of God. Members of the local church hold a responsibility towards one another. They are to spur each other on toward good works and exhort one another to live consistent lives worthy of God. Believers are commanded not to neglect the assembling of themselves together.

"Let us think of ways to motivate one another to acts of love and good works. And let us not neglect our meeting together, as some people do, but encourage one another, especially now that the day of his return is drawing near."

– Hebrews 10:24-25 (NLT)

Hebrews 10:24-25 encourages believers to consider how to spur one another on toward love and good deeds, not giving up meeting together but encouraging one another. It emphasizes the importance of community support and gathering together in faith.

"They worshiped together at the Temple each day, met in homes for the Lord's Supper, and shared their meals with great joy and generosity all the while praising God and enjoying the goodwill of all the people. And each day the Lord added to their fellowship those who were being saved."

— Acts 2:46-47 (NLT)

The early Christian community is described in Acts 2:46-47. They met daily with glad and sincere hearts, praising God and enjoying favor with all the people. Every day, the Lord added to their number those who were being saved. The church grew in numbers and in unity.

Sharing Our Faith

Sharing our faith in Christ with those who have not experienced new life in Him is a command of God. This demonstrates our love for God. Christ said that if we truly loved Him, we would keep His commandments.

"Therefore, go and make disciples of all the nations, baptizing them in the name of the Father and the Son and the Holy Spirit. Teach these new disciples to obey all the commands I have given you. And be sure of this: I am with you always, even to the end of the age."

— Matthew 28:19-20 (NLT)

Known as the Great Commission given in Matthew 28:19-20, Jesus instructed His disciples to go and make disciples of all nations, baptizing them and teaching them to obey all that He commanded. He also made a promise that He would always be with them.

"But you will receive power when the Holy Spirit comes upon you. And you will be my witnesses, telling people about me everywhere—in Jerusalem, throughout Judea, in Samaria, and to the ends of the earth."

– Acts 1:8 (NLT)

In Acts 1:8, Jesus told His disciples that they would receive power when the Holy Spirit came upon them and they would be His witnesses in Jerusalem, and in all Judea and Samaria, and to the ends of the earth. This verse speaks to the empowering of all believers through the Holy Spirit for mission work.

Walking in the Spirit

The Bible describes Christian life as "walking in the Spirit" (Galatians 5:16). Walking best represents the step-by-step character of the spiritual life. Living by the Spirit's power is a moment-by-moment yielding to His will and control.

The evidence that we are walking in the Spirit is simply the display of the fruit of the Spirit (Galatians 5:22-23). Walking in the Spirit involves confessing our sin, yielding to God by obeying the Word of God, and being filled with and controlled by the Spirit.

"Don't be drunk with wine, because that will ruin your life. Instead, be filled with the Holy Spirit, singing psalms and hymns and spiritual songs among yourselves, and making music to the Lord in your hearts."

– Ephesians 5:18-19 (NLT)

In Ephesians 5:18-19, Paul advised believers not to get drunk on wine but to be filled with the Spirit, speaking to one another with psalms, hymns, and songs from the Spirit. This encourages joyful expression and spiritual fellowship among believers.

> "After this prayer, the meeting place shook, and they were all filled with the Holy Spirit. Then they preached the word of God with boldness."
>
> – Acts 4:31 (NLT)

After the believers prayed in Acts 4:31, their meeting place was shaken, they were all filled with the Holy Spirit, and spoke the word of God boldly.

Problems in the New Life

Just as we have problems in our physical life, we also experience difficulties in our spiritual or new life. Facing and conquering these challenges leads to growth and inner strength, whether they are physical or spiritual in nature. As we grow in this newfound strength, we bring glory to God by showcasing His faithfulness and the sufficiency of His grace for all our needs.

> Each time he said, "My grace is all you need. My power works best in weakness."
>
> – 2 Corinthians 12:9 (NLT)

We read in 2 Corinthians 12:9 where Paul recounted God's response to his plea for relief from a "thorn in his flesh."(verse 7) God promised to provide strength during times of personal weakness.

The process of strengthening one's faith is best accomplished by reading and understanding the Word of God (Romans 10:17). The Holy Spirit convicts the willing heart of His power. Growing in God's Word results in the growth of faith.

Reading and understanding the Word are like planting seeds of faith in the heart. These seeds will bear the mature fruit of faith.

A Changed Life

Without a doubt, the greatest proof of the new birth is a changed life. The child of God now suddenly loves the following:

- **He loves Jesus.**

Before conversion, the sinner might hold Christ in high esteem, but after conversion, he loves the Saviour.

"Everyone who believes that Jesus is the Christ has become a child of God. And everyone who loves the Father loves his children, too. We know we love God's children if we love God and obey his commandments."

– 1 John 5:1-2 (NLT)

The passage found in 1 John 5:1-2 states that everyone who believes that Jesus is the Christ is born of God, and everyone who loves the Father loves His child as well. It connects belief in Jesus to being part of God's family and loving others.

- **He loves the Bible.**

We should love God's Word as the psalmist King David did. In the Book of Psalms, he expresses his great love for God's Word.

"How I delight in your commands! How I love them! I honor and love your commands. I meditate on your decrees."

— Psalm 119:47-48 (NLT)

"How sweet your words taste to me; they are sweeter than honey. Your commandments give me understanding; no wonder I hate every false way of life. Your word is a lamp to guide my feet and a light for my path."

— Psalm 119:103-105 (NLT)

These words found in Psalm 119:47-48 and 103-105 express delight and love for God's commands, describing them as the sweet taste of honey and as a lamp to the feet and a light to the path. They highlight the joy and guidance found in following God's Word.

- **He loves other Christians.**

We should love our Christian brothers and sisters as we are all one in Christ.

If we love our brothers and sisters who are believers,it proves that we have passed from death to life. But a person who has no love is still dead. Anyone who hates another brother or sister is really a murderer at heart. And you know that murderers don't have eternal life within them.

— 1 John 3:14-15 (NLT)

1 John 3:14-15 states that passing from death to life is evidenced by loving other believers. It is a serious offense for those who do not love. It's as if they are existing in death. Anyone who hates a brother is as guilty as a murderer, without eternal life. Hate carries severe spiritual consequences.

- **He loves his enemies.**

We were all created by God in His own image, and God loves everyone. He hates the sin, but not the sinner. Therefore, we must show love even to our enemies.

"You have heard that it was said, 'Love your neighbor and hate your enemy.' But I tell you, love your enemies and pray for those who persecute you, that you may be children of your Father in heaven. He causes his sun to rise on the evil and the good, and sends rain on the righteous and the unrighteous."

– Matthew 5:43-45 (NIV)

Jesus taught us to love our enemies and pray for those who persecute us in Matthew 5:43-45. He explained that this behavior reflects the character of the Father in heaven. This teaching is part of Jesus' emphasis on surpassing the traditional understanding of love and extending it to all people, including enemies.

- **He loves the souls of all people.**

Like Paul, we can cry out for the conversion of loved ones. He expressed his heart's desire and prayer to God for Israel in Romans 10:1. He longed for them to be saved.

"Brothers and sisters, my heart's desire and prayer to God for the Israelites is that they may be saved."

– Romans 10:1 (NIV)

"For Christ's love compels us..."

– 2 Corinthians 5:14 (NIV)

In 2 Corinthians 5:14, Paul wrote that Christ's love compels or drives us, since we are convinced that One died for all, and therefore all died. This verse speaks to the motivational force of Christ's love in the believer's life, driving them towards selfless actions and perspectives.

- **He loves the pure life.**

The Spirit of God enables him to lead a holy and pure life, always desiring to please God in all his actions.

"Do not love the world or anything in the world. If anyone loves the world, love for the Father is not in them."

— 1 John 2:15 (NIV)

John warns in 1 John 2:15 against loving the world or anything in the world, stating that if anyone loves the world, the love of the Father is not in them. It reflects the distinction between divine love and worldly desires.

"For everyone born of God overcomes the world. This is the victory that has overcome the world, even our faith. Who is it that overcomes the world? Only the one who believes that Jesus is the Son of God."

— 1 John 5:4-5 (NIV)

1 John 3:14-15 states that passing from death to life is evidenced by loving fellow believers. It is a serious offense for those who do not love. It's as if they are existing in death. Anyone who hates a brother is as guilty as a murderer, without eternal life. Hate carries severe spiritual consequences.

1 John 5:4-5 proclaims that everyone born of God overcomes the world, and this victory is achieved through our faith. Whoever believes that Jesus is the Son of God overcomes the world. It emphasizes the power of faith in Jesus to overcome worldly challenges and influences.

- **He loves to talk to God.**

His relationship with God is so close that he prefers prayer and talking to God over worldly matters.

"addressing one another in psalms and hymns and spiritual songs, singing and making melody to the Lord with your heart, giving thanks always and for everything to God the Father in the name of our Lord Jesus Christ,"

– Ephesians 5:19-20 (ESV)

According to Ephesians 5:19-20, Paul advises speaking to one another with psalms, hymns, and songs from the Spirit, singing and making music from the heart to the Lord, always giving thanks to God the Father for everything. This passage encourages joyful expression of faith and constant gratitude.

SHARING YOUR FAITH AND TESTIMONY

PART 3

God Created You

You were created by a loving God. You have great value. God loves you and wants to have a personal relationship with you.

God knew you before you were born—even while you were in your mother's womb. He knew all about your family and your life until now. He wants to give you a brand new start and a new way of living. He can do that when you give him your life.

"You made all the delicate, inner parts of my body and knit me together in my mother's womb. Thank you for making me so wonderfully complex! Your workmanship is marvelous – how well I knew it. You watched me as I was being formed in utter seclusion, as I was woven together in the dark of the womb. You saw me before I was born. Every day of my life was recorded in your book. Every moment was laid out before a single day had passed."

– Psalm 139:13-16 (NLT)

God Loves You

You can turn your life over to God's control because He loves you and wants the very best for you. In fact, He loves you so much that He gave His Son, Jesus, to die on the cross for you. When you trust God, you are actually trusting the One who created you. When you turn your life over to Him, you are giving your life to the One who knows you inside and out.

> "For God loved the world so much that he gave his one and only Son, so that everyone who believes in him will not perish but have eternal life."
>
> – John 3:16 (NLT)

John 3:16 declares that God loved the world so much that He gave His only Son, so that whoever believes in Him should not perish but have eternal life. It emphasizes God's love and the gift of salvation through belief in Jesus.

God wants to have a personal relationship with you

God is not some "force," an unspeaking or unseeing idol, or merely another name for your own self-esteem. Instead, God is a person, your Creator, who created you to be in relationship with Him. He created you in His own image.

> "Jesus replied, 'All who love me will do what I say. My Father will love them, and we will come and make our home with each of them. Anyone who doesn't love me will not obey me. And remember, my words are not my own. What I am telling you is from the Father who sent me. I am telling you these things now while I am still with you. But when the Father sends the Advocate

as my representative—that is, the Holy Spirit—he will teach you everything and will remind you of everything I have told you.'"

– John 14:23-25 (NLT)

Jesus explained that anyone who loves Him will obey His teaching, and God will love them and make His home with them. John 14:23-25 speaks to the intimate relationship between God and those who follow Jesus' teachings, promising the Holy Spirit as a helper and teacher.

Sin keeps you from having a personal relationship with God

Your sin keeps you from having a relationship with the Creator, God. God is holy and perfect; people are sinful. The Bible says that "everyone has sinned" (Romans 3:23). We simply cannot help it–we're human. When Adam and Eve sinned way back in the Garden of Eden, sin entered the human race. Sinfulness is now part of our nature.

Because God is holy and perfect, and we are sinners, He cannot have anything to do with us. That is why Jesus came into this world. It's only through Jesus Christ that you can have a personal relationship with God.

"For the sin of this one man, Adam, caused death to rule over many."

– Romans 5:17 (NLT)

Paul writes in Romans 5:17 that death reigned through one man, Adam. But believers will enjoy life all the more because of Jesus Christ. This verse contrasts the consequences of Adam's sin with the grace found in Christ.

"For everyone has sinned; we all fall short of God's glorious standard."

— Romans 3:23 (NLT)

Romans 3:23 states that everyone has sinned and falls short of the glory of God.

"Jesus said: 'I am the way, the truth, and the life. No one can come to the Father except through me.'"

— John 14:6 (NLT)

Jesus declares that He is the way, the truth, and the life, and no one comes to the Father except through Him. John 14:6 emphasizes the exclusive nature of salvation only through Jesus.

Why Jesus Christ?

Jesus died to bear the penalty our sins deserved. In essence, He took our punishment upon Himself so that we need not face punishment. Now, because of Jesus, the way is prepared for us to have a personal relationship with a holy God.

In the Old Testament, people sacrificed animals as a way to show how sorry they were for their sins. God the Father chose to address our sins by sending His perfect son, Jesus, as the final and ultimate sacrifice for all of humanity.

Christ suffered for our sins once and for all, and He, who never sinned, did so to secure the safe return of sinners to God. He endured physical death but was raised to life in the Spirit. (1 Peter 3:18)

You must respond personally by trusting Jesus Christ as Savior and Lord. The fact of salvation means nothing unless a person accepts it for themselves. Even if individuals grew up in church, they still need to personally accept Jesus.

Even if someone has lived a terribly sinful life, he is not too bad for God. A person does not have to "clean up his act" before coming to Christ. Jesus died to remove all sin and provide a fresh start. Simply being good is not good enough, yet no one is too far gone to receive forgiveness. God wants all people to come to Him. All people must completely trust in Jesus to be saved.

On your own, you cannot be good enough for a perfect God. When you recognize that you are indeed a sinner in need of a Savior, simply believe.

> "But to all who believed him and accepted him, he gave the right to become children of God."
>
> – John 1:12 (NLT)

John explains in chapter one, verse twelve that to all who did receive Jesus, to those who believed in His name, He gave the right to become children of God. This verse highlights the life-changing power of believing in Jesus.

> "If you confess with your mouth that Jesus is Lord and believe in your heart that God raised him from the dead, you will be saved. For it is by believing in your heart that you are made right with God, and it is by confessing with your mouth that you are saved."
>
> – Romans 10: 9-10 (NLT)

Paul teaches in Romans 10:9-10 that if you confess with your mouth that Jesus is Lord and believe in your heart that God raised Him from the dead, you will be saved. Confession and belief are both necessary for salvation.

"Receiving Christ" involves acknowledging your belief in Him, inviting Him into your life, repenting, and turning away from your current way of living, and beginning a NEW LIFE in which you allow God to guide every aspect of your existence. The moment you ask, it's done. Jesus has come in!

Would you like to accept Jesus as your Savior?

Prayer is just talking to God. He knows what you mean even when you are unable to express yourself in words. You may use your own words or you can repeat the following simple prayer:

> Dear God, I know I'm a sinner, and my sins have separated me from you. I thank you for Jesus Christ, Who died on the cross in my place. Lord Jesus, please forgive my sins and come into my life. Take control of my life as I surrender to You completely. Thank You for giving me eternal life. In Jesus' name, Amen.

That's it! You are now a new believer in God's family. May God bless you.

Placed into God's Family

In a general sense, all men and women are the children of God, as He is the Creator. However, this relationship is not sufficient to offset the penalty of sin, because all people are sinners separated from God.

> "For everyone has sinned; we all fall short of God's glorious standard."
>
> — Romans 3:23 (NLT)

Therefore, for a sinful person to become a child of God, a miraculous transformation must take place. The Bible refers to this change as being "born again." When an individual places his faith in Christ as Saviour, he is born again into a new, spiritual, family relationship with God. He gains God as Father and other Christians as brothers and sisters. Not only are Christians the children of God by spiritual birth; they are adopted as well. One is no longer in bondage to the master but becomes a free son, possessing all the rights and privileges of sonship.

> "For you are all children of God through faith in Christ Jesus."
>
> – Galatians 3:26 (NLT)

In Galatians 3:26, Paul states that in Christ Jesus, all are children of God through faith.

One of these benefits is the right to call God "Abba," an affectionate term meaning "father." This marvelous relationship carries both responsibilities and privileges. Since one bears the family relationship to God, he must also exhibit the family character.

> "And because we are his children, God has sent the Spirit of his Son into our hearts, prompting us to call out, "Abba, Father." Now you are no longer a slave but God's own child.And since you are his child, God has made you his heir.
>
> – Galatians 4:6-7 (NLT)

Galatians 4:6-7 explains that because believers are God's children, God sent the Spirit of His Son into their hearts. Therefore, believers are no longer slaves but God's children, and since they are His children, they are also heirs. This passage speaks to the intimate relationship of believers with God and their spiritual inheritance.

> "So you have not received a spirit that makes you fearful slaves. Instead, you received God's Spirit when he adopted you as his own children. Now we call him, "Abba, Father." For his Spirit joins with our spirit to affirm that we are God's children."

> — Romans 8:15-16 (NLT)

Believers have not received a spirit that makes them fearful slaves, but they have received God's Spirit, and by Him, they call God "Abba, Father." In Romans 8:15-16, the Holy Spirit Himself testifies with their spirit that they are God's children. It emphasizes the close and personal relationship believers have with God.

God the Father of Believers

God is the Father of believers also in the sense that He gives them new life. This relationship, then, is a family one involving many of the same realities that exist between an earthly father and child; birth of the child; partaking of the father's nature; the father's care of the child; and the father's discipline of the child. Furthermore, this new Father-child relationship carries with it new brothers and sisters.

To obtain God as Father is not a result of one's own merit but a result of Christ's death on the cross. The one who believes in Christ as Saviour enters into the blessed Father-child relationship with God, solely on the grounds of Christ's Sonship. It is the grand privilege and calling of those who know God as Father to graciously invite unbelievers to meet God as Father and not as Judge.

"And if children, then heirs; heirs of God, and joint-heirs with Christ; if indeed we suffer with him, that we may also be glorified together."

— Romans 8:17 (NIV)

Romans 8:17 explains that if we are children of God, we are also heirs—heirs of God and co-heirs with Christ, sharing in His sufferings and glory. It highlights the believers' spiritual inheritance and identification with Christ.

Believers are Empowered by God

A believer who has gained the sonship of God the Father is also empowered by God to serve Him and glorify His holy name. God provides the power to live the Christian life. All Christians are indwelt by the Spirit and thus have His power available in specific instances such as sharing their faith with others, resisting temptation, remaining faithful, and more. It is simply a reliance on the Spirit to receive help.

"But you will receive power when the Holy Spirit comes on you; and you will be my witnesses in Jerusalem, and in all Judea and Samaria, and to the ends of the earth."

— Acts 1:8 (NIV)

Jesus tells His disciples that they will receive power when the Holy Spirit comes on them and they will be His witnesses to the ends of the earth. (Acts 1:8)

"With great power the apostles continued to testify to the resurrection of the Lord Jesus. And God's grace was so powerfully at work in them all"

— Acts 4:33 (NIV)

The apostles are described as giving testimony to the resurrection of the Lord Jesus with great power. Acts 4:33 shows the boldness and effectiveness of the early Christian witness.

> "Do you not know that your bodies are temples of the Holy Spirit, who is in you, whom you have received from God? You are not your own; you were bought at a price. Therefore honor God with your bodies."
>
> – 1 Corinthians 6:19-20 (NIV)

In 1 Corinthians 6:19-20, Paul reminds believers that their bodies are temples of the Holy Spirit and they were bought at a price. Therefore, they should honor God with their bodies, recognizing their value and purpose.

Enemies trying to defeat Christians

Three powerful enemies are constantly trying to defeat the Christian's testimony and spiritual success:

- The World

- The Flesh

- The Devil

Temptation by the World:

> "because all that is in the world (the desire of the flesh and the desire of the eyes and the arrogance produced by material possessions) is not from the Father, but is from the world."
>
> -1 John 2:16 (NET)

John warns against loving the world or the things in the world, describing the desires of the flesh, the desires of the eyes, and the pride of life as not from the Father but from the world. We read about this in 1 John 2:16.

> "We know that we are from God, and the whole world lies in the power of the evil one."
>
> – 1 John 5:19 (NET)

According to 1 John 5:19, the whole world is under the control of the evil one, highlighting the spiritual battle and the influence of evil in the world.

The temptations for the believer are twofold: the lure of sensual desires and the pride of mastering one's own life. The world's attraction is amplified by Satan, known as the "prince of this world," and it's said that the entire world is under his power.

Some of the tragic effects that the love of the world will produce in the believer's life are:

- **A turning away from the Lord's work and other believers**

> "Demas has deserted me because he loves the things of this life and has gone to Thessalonica. Crescens has gone to Galatia, and Titus has gone to Dalmatia."
>
> – 2 Timothy 4:10 (NLT)

Paul laments in 2 Timothy 4:10 that Demas, because of his love for this world, had deserted him. This serves as a caution against being enticed away from spiritual commitments by worldly allure.

- **Alienation from God**

> "You adulterers! Don't you realize that friendship with the world makes you an enemy of God? I say it again:

If you want to be a friend of the world, you make yourself an enemy of God."

— James 4:4 (NLT)

In James 4:4, the author equates friendship with the world as enmity with God, stating that whoever chooses to be a friend of the world becomes an enemy of God.

- **Corrupting sins**

  "And because of his glory and excellence, he has given us great and precious promises. These are the promises that enable you to share his divine nature and escape the world's corruption caused by human desires."

  — 2 Peter 1:4 (NLT)

2 Peter 1:4 speaks of the great and precious promises given to believers, through which they may participate in the divine nature and escape the corruption in the world caused by evil desires.

- **Deception by false teachers**

  "Dear friends, do not believe everyone who claims to speak by the Spirit. You must test them to see if the spirit they have comes from God. For there are many false prophets in the world."

  — 1 John 4:1 (NLT)

In his first epistle, chapter four and verse 1, John advises believers not to believe every spirit. Instead, they must test them to see whether they are from God, as many false prophets have gone out into the world.

The solution to overcoming the love of the world is to have a greater love for the Father. Christians who seek to please God daily in everything, striving for spiritual growth through prayer, studying God's Word, and witnessing, need not fall prey to the temptations of the world.

Temptation by the Flesh:

"The flesh" means something other than the substance of the human body; it refers to the carnal, sinful principle within man that is opposed to God. The actions produced by the flesh are given in detail in Galatians 5:19-21, and among these are all types of sexual immorality, impurity, hatred, anger, false religions, envy, and drunkenness. A person whose life is characterized by these sins cannot be a true Christian and is under the wrath of God.

A Christian possesses a new nature empowered by the Holy Spirit. Since the flesh and the Spirit are in total opposition to each other, the one that the believer allows to dominate him will take charge in his life and produce its own fruit.

> "The mind governed by the flesh is hostile to God; it does not submit to God's law, nor can it do so. Those who are in the realm of the flesh cannot please God."
>
> – Romans 8:7-8 (NIV)

In Romans 8:7-8, Paul explains that the mind governed by the flesh is hostile to God, does not submit to God's law, and cannot please God, highlighting the conflict between the sinful nature and God's will.

> "All of us also lived among them at one time, gratifying the cravings of our flesh and following its desires and thoughts. Like the rest, we were by nature deserving of wrath."
>
> – Ephesians 2:3 (NIV)

A passage we find in Ephesians 2:3 describes how we all once lived gratifying the cravings of the flesh, following its desires and thoughts. Because of this we deserved wrath.

The solution to the urges of the flesh lies in recognizing that the power of sin was nullified by Jesus' death on the cross and in living under the control of the Spirit's power. The believer must choose, by an act of their will, to benefit from the Spirit's enablement, which is a moment-by-moment dependence on the power of the Holy Spirit through faith.

> "In the same way, count yourselves dead to sin but alive to God in Christ Jesus. Therefore do not let sin reign in your mortal body so that you obey its evil desires."
>
> — Romans 6:11-12 (NIV)

Paul urges believers to consider themselves dead to sin but alive to God in Christ Jesus, and not to let sin reign in their mortal bodies. We find this in Romans 6:11-12.

Temptation by Satan:

Satan stands opposed to all the work of God and promotes defiance among men. His role against Christians is to deceive them, accuse them, devour their testimony for Christ, hinder their work for God, and tempt them to immorality. He is also called "the devil," which means "accuser." He can appear as a hideous dragon or as a beautifully deceptive "angel of light."

> "For such people are false apostles, deceitful workers, masquerading as apostles of Christ. And no wonder, for Satan himself masquerades as an angel of light. It is not surprising, then, if his servants also masquerade

as servants of righteousness. Their end will be what their actions deserve."

– 2 Corinthians 11:13-14 (NIV)

In 2 Corinthians 11:13-14, Paul warns about false apostles who disguise themselves as apostles of Christ. He notes that this is not surprising, as even Satan disguises himself as an angel of light. This passage highlights the reality of deceitful workers in the Christian community, masquerading as servants of righteousness.

In 2 Corinthians 11:13-14, Paul warns about false apostles who disguise themselves as apostles of Christ. He notes that this is not surprising, as even Satan disguises himself as an angel of light. This passage highlights the reality of deceitful workers in the Christian community, masquerading as servants of righteousness.

The terrifying work of Satan in unbelievers is described in Scripture as follows: he blinds their minds; he takes the word of God from their hearts, and he controls them.

"And these are the ones along the path, where the word is sown: when they hear, Satan immediately comes and takes away the word that is sown in them."

– Mark 4:15 (ESV)

Mark 4:15 outlines part of Jesus' explanation of the Parable of the Sower. He describes how, when some people hear the Word, Satan comes immediately and takes away the Word that was sown in them. It points to the spiritual opposition that attempts to prevent people from accepting and understanding God's Word.

A Christian must be able to recognize the power and deception of Satan and adhere steadfastly to the faith, openly resisting him and not giving him opportunities for any temptation. The best way to oppose him is to be a growing Christian, spending time studying the Word of God, being at the feet of our Lord in prayer, and having times of fasting. Then, a believer can respond to Satan's temptations with confidence, knowing that nothing can separate them from the love of God.

> "Stay alert! Watch out for your great enemy, the devil. He prowls around like a roaring lion, looking for someone to devour. Stand firm against him, and be strong in your faith. Remember that your family of believers all over the world is going through the same kind of suffering you are."
>
> - 1 Peter 5:8-9 (NLT)

SHARING YOUR FAITH AND TESTIMONY

PART 4

Evangelism

In 1 Peter 5:8-9, Peter advises believers to be alert and of sober mind because their enemy, the devil, prowls around like a roaring lion looking for someone to devour. He encourages them to resist him, standing firm in the faith, and to be aware that believers throughout the world are undergoing the same kinds of suffering. This passage emphasizes the need for vigilance against spiritual threats and the encouragement that comes from knowing others share the same struggles.

Evangelism is the duty of all Christians. The great commission at the end of Matthew's gospel is a commission for all who follow Jesus Christ: "Therefore go and make disciples of all nations, baptizing them in the name of the Father and of the Son and of the Holy Spirit" (Matthew 28:19, NIV).

As Christians, there are four reasons for us to share our faith. The first three are related to our duty.

1. Christ commands us to do this.

2. The world urgently needs the gospel.

3. The fields are already "ripe for harvest."
   – John 4:35 (NIV)

4. The fourth reason relates to our own spiritual health. We share our faith because we cannot contain ourselves. This was true of the early church. When the religious authorities ordered the disciples to stop preaching the gospel, Peter's answer described their burning desire:

   > "For we cannot help speaking about what we have seen and heard." – Acts 4:20 (NIV)

Acts 4:20 finds Peter and John explaining that they cannot help but speak about what they have seen and heard. This statement is made in the context of them being commanded not to speak or teach in the name of Jesus. It underscores the apostles' commitment to boldly proclaiming the truth of the gospel, regardless of opposition or commands to the contrary.

Evangelism is not a matter of knowing all the answers, nor does it require that we have a sophisticated theological argument. Instead, it is a natural outgrowth of a deep faith that drives Christians to share their faith. It is something good that we want others to enjoy.

The Rewards of Sharing

What a joy and privilege it is to share in the process of leading one lost person to God, to experience the rejoicing with the angels over a lost sinner found, to have the inner satisfaction of having been used by God, and to share in the deep satisfaction of seeing God's kingdom extended in our patch.

The Blessings of Sharing

There are blessings to us when we share our faith as well. It serves as a purpose for the very reason that God has given us life. If we don't pass on the faith to the next generation, both they and our faith will die together..

Christ entrusted the Gospel into the hands of regular people, like fishermen and tax collectors—sinners just like us—and saved us.

God has a plan and a purpose for every encounter we have throughout a given day or week. Sharing our faith brings fulfillment.

Nothing feels better than accomplishing something you've been called for, trained for, and equipped for by God.

Satisfaction of Sharing

The satisfaction of a runner completing a marathon or a doctor healing a patient can be likened to the immense joy we experience when we fulfill God's purpose for sharing our faith.

Sharing our faith helps us to grow in our faith.

There is a saying: **"If you want to really learn something, teach it to others."**

We grow in our faith when we turn to God in prayer before we witness to others. We also grow as we learn how to handle objections and questions presented to us. We grow as the Holy Spirit encourages us by residing within us and doing the work. Finally, we grow in our confidence as we defend what we believe and why we believe it.

Honor of Sharing

Sharing our faith is an honor that God has reserved for us. There is nothing else in all of creation that has been given this privilege.

But most of all, I think, it is the investment we're making in storing up treasures in Heaven. Nothing we do in this world will last for eternity except those things pertaining to faith. The joy we'll realize when we've been used by God to save another precious soul and the eternal thanks we'll receive from those we've helped bring to Christ are immeasurable blessings.

We are NOT witnesses by compulsion or by expectation!

We will be witnesses as we are inwardly motivated by our love of Christ,

"The expulsive power of a new affection!"

Accept Your Calling

Jesus, today I accept my calling
not to perfection or performance.
My calling is to faith.
I have been chosen for this generation.
I have a place in the heritage of faith.
I'm going to stop wishing and whining
and start believing and receiving.
What Your Word says is mine.
I won't let others steal my hope.
I won't argue with a Pharisee.
I will believe and therefore speak,
for You, my God, are huge.
Nothing is too hard for You.
Our world needs Your wonders.
Rise up, oh Lord!
Please renew Your works in our day.
I confess the unbelief of my generation
and ask You to begin Your revival of faith
in my own heart.
For You are who You say You are.
You can do what You say You can do.
I am who You say I am.
I can do all things through Christ.
Your Word is alive and active in me.
Satan, hear me clearly:
My Father is Maker of heaven and earth.
You are under my feet, today and the rest of my days, because
I'm believing in God!
And
I will share my Faith.

Dear Brothers & Sisters in Christ!

Let us, as Christians, join hands to be witnesses to the people around us and share our faith to win many souls, establishing the Kingdom of God on earth and preparing the way for the soon coming of our Lord and Savior, Jesus Christ.

Commission

Give us a watchword for the hour,
A thrilling word, a word of power;
A battle cry, a flaming breath,
A call to conquest or to death;
A word to rouse the church from rest,
To heed the Master's high behest.
The call is given, ye hosts arise,
The watchword is EVANGELIZE!
To fallen men, a dying race,
Make known the gift of gospel grace.
The world that now in darkness lies,
O Church of Christ, EVANGELIZE!!

MORE FROM
PASTOR ALFRED

PASTOR • SERVANT • AUTHOR

alfred-cherubim.com

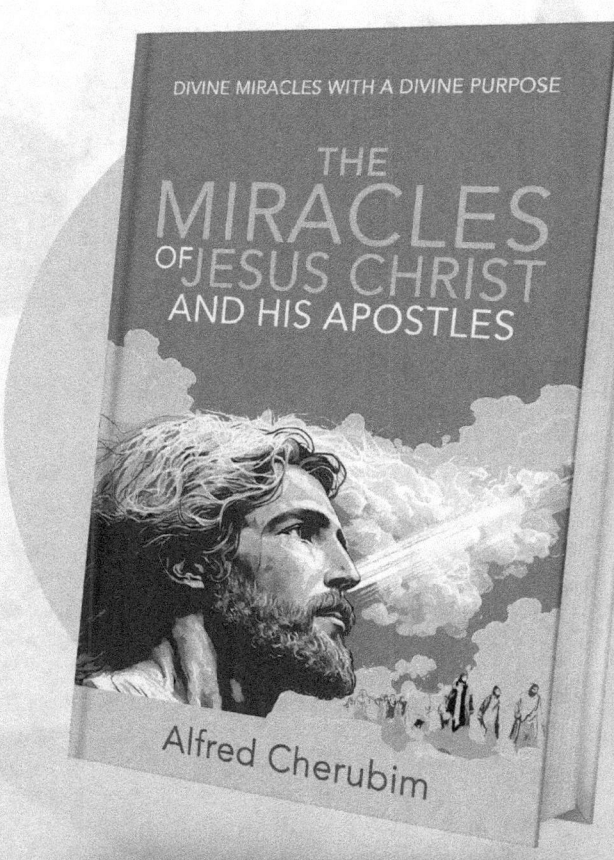

Experience the Power of Divine Miracles with
Jesus and His Apostles through

The Miracles of Jesus Christ and His Apostles in the Bible: Divine Miracles with a Divine Purpose

SHARING YOUR FAITH AND TESTIMONY introduces Pastor S. Alfred Cherubim's incredible journey from doubt to transformative encounters with Jesus. This book celebrates God's power, highlighting moments like overcoming a heart attack and awakening from a coma. It shares moving stories of healing from severe eczema and chronic rheumatic paralysis. Beyond these experiences, the book explores timeless Bible truths, emphasizing the Christian mission of sharing faith. Learn how sharing stories about Jesus invites others into His transformative love. Be inspired, prepared, and challenged to share your own testimony passionately through this book, and continue spreading the word about Jesus with purpose.

PASTOR S. ALFRED CHERUBIM'S life journey takes him from Sri Lanka to Canada, where he has worked as an Agricultural Officer and held key positions in the YMCA Movement. In the midst of healing moments and meetings with Jesus, he was confronted with the difficult aftermath of ethnic violence, leading to his departure from Sri Lanka in 1983. Fortunately, neither he nor his family were harmed. He continued his career with the YMCA in India until entering full-time ministry in 1990. He then returned to Sri Lanka and established an orphanage for Children who have been impacted by ethnic disputes. As the present pastor of the Redeemer Christ Assembly Church in Canada, Pastor Cherubim is witnessing 25 years of devoted ministry, a testimonial to the growing power of faith and the global mission of spreading the Word of Jesus.

ISBN 978-1-961614-78-9

90000

SPIRIT MEDIA

9 781961 614789